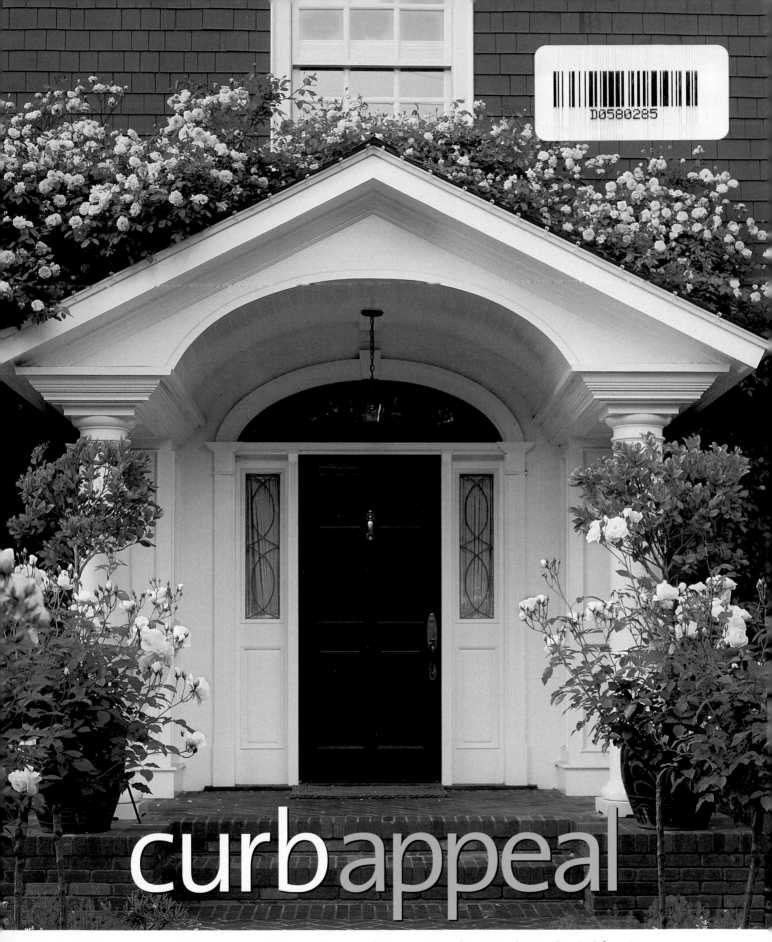

curbappeal

By Don Vandervort and the Editors of Sunset Books, Menlo Park, California

Sunset Books

VP and General Manager: Richard A. Smeby
VP and Editorial Director: Bob Doyle
Production Director: Lory Day
Operations Director: Rosann Sutherland
Retail Sales Development Manager: Linda Barker
Executive Editor: Bridget Biscotti Bradley
Art Director: Vasken Guiragossian
Special Sales: Brad Moses

Curb Appeal was produced
in conjunction with HomeTips, Inc.

Editor: Don Vandervort
Managing Editor: Louise Damberg
Assistant Editor: Gabriel Vandervort
Graphic Designer: Daniel Nadeau
Contributing Editors: Carol A. Crotta,
          Patricia L. Freeman
Production Coordinator: Eligio Hernandez
Copy Editor: Kristinha Anding
Editorial Assistant: Emily Lerner
Index: Rick Hurd, Rick's Indexing

Cover: Photography by Thomas J. Story (top,
bottom right), Robert Benson (bottom middle),
and John Granen (bottom left).

For additional copies of *Curb Appeal* or any other
Sunset book, call 1-800-526-5111 or visit us at
www.sunsetbooks.com

Contents

Makeover Projects

Curb Appeal

Have you ever noticed that certain houses are undeniably attractive at first glance? Something sets them apart—a quality that isn't always as obvious as a new coat of paint or a lush green lawn. That is curb appeal.

The term "curb appeal" originated within the lexicon of real estate professionals, a reference to surface improvements that help a house to sell quickly. But now the term has come to mean much more. Today, it refers to a house that is well maintained, true to its architectural style, beautifully landscaped, accented with details, and more.

Does your home have it? Next time you drive up your street, look at your house as if you're seeing it for the first time. What catches your eye? Does your home look loved and taken care of and proud to be a member of the neighborhood? Or does it look a bit sad? Do you see problems such as worn paint, colors that are out of sync with each other, and landscaping that is a hodgepodge of overgrown plantings?

Your house may need just a bit of inspiration or sprucing up, or it may need new siding, a new paint job, or a landscaping overhaul. Whatever the improvements, this book will help you make them happen.

First Impressions, the initial chapter, is full of creative ideas and helpful advice for brainstorming and focusing on the improvements that are appropriate for your home.

Then, when you turn to the second chapter, Makeover Workbook, roll up your sleeves. This section discusses how to find and work with professionals and how to make informed buying decisions about specific products and materials. You will also find many improvement projects that include step-by-step directions for doing your own work.

BEFORE & AFTER A quality paint job, landscaping, and thoughtful details transformed this plain-Jane house into the pride of the neighborhood.

Ideas, inspiration, hands-on knowledge—with these tools, your home may become the most beautiful house on the block!

First Impressions

Making the front of your home look warm and inviting and ensuring that it reflects your family's personality can be a fun and rewarding challenge. The process is a bit like creating a piece of artwork—you bring together design elements such as color, texture, and form and blend them into a result that is cohesive, interesting, and, when done well, downright beautiful.

If you have decided that your home could use a little—or perhaps a lot—of help in the curb appeal department but you're not sure where to begin, you've come to the right place. This chapter is loaded with helpful advice and photographic examples of the types of improvements that can make a big difference in how your home looks and functions. The following pages will help you understand the role that design elements play in making successful improvements and will give you plenty of great ideas to spark and inspire your own creative efforts.

How can you capitalize on your home's architecture in the design of your improvements? How large or small a project should you try to tackle? This chapter will help you sort through these and other issues. Here you can explore the use of color and discover ways of creating appealing entries, porches, driveways, and more. You will also find examples and advice on how to use landscaping and hardscaping effectively, how to blend your house with its site, and how to carve out a front-yard entertaining space. And, as the proverbial icing on the cake, this chapter discusses the decorative details and whimsical improvements that will set your house apart from the rest.

BEFORE & AFTER
From beast to beauty: Makeover advice is illustrated by remodels before and after their transformations.

Sweet harmony—of form, materials, colors, textures, accents, and natural elements— makes this house a neighborhood standout.

Ever notice that, on almost any given block of houses, one stands out? It is not a matter of size—that house may not be as big as some others. No, it is something else that makes that house so appealing.

If you can't put your finger on exactly what it is that attracts you to a house, most likely it's because everything works together. The property exudes a sense of pride. The home owners have thoughtfully put together a package of details— architecture, paint, trim, accessories, and landscaping—that complement one another and blend seamlessly into a perfect whole. It's no wonder that this house has, as they say, good vibes and a natural curb appeal.

Whether you are interested in a quick sprucing up of your home's exterior or a massive makeover, certain principles remain the same. Your overall design scheme, to be successful, must be cohesive, harmonious, and true to the architecture of your home. Think of it as a house of cards—each card relating to and supporting the others. The more hodgepodge the individual elements, the less each element will complement the others and the worse the property will look overall. Yet, harmony does not mean cookie-cutter blandness. A well-placed bit of contrast—an unusual trim color, choice of fencing, or creative landscaping—can elevate a nice house into something truly special: a house with personality.

A well-designed house will seem unique, but all well-designed houses share certain characteristics:

■ They are well sited on the property and integrate well with the other houses on the block.

■ The mass of the house itself is broken up and arranged pleasingly into connecting, well-proportioned shapes. The exceptions to this, of course, are architectural styles that are boxy by definition—Georgian and Colonial, for example.

■ Windows, interesting architectural focal points in their own right, are generous and well-proportioned.

■ The materials used throughout the property are of good quality, are appropriate to the house's architectural style, and create an interesting interplay of textures.

■ The hues of the color scheme—from roof to walls, to trim and accents, to landscaping—complement and contrast well with each other and are eye-catching.

■ The landscaping provides another layer of shapes to accentuate or counterpoint the architecture and the color scheme. All plantings are thoughtfully chosen, well tended, and well pruned to maintain proper proportion to the house.

■ The pathway and front door are easy to locate, well lit for night use, and welcoming.

■ Accessories—architectural embellishments, front-yard garden structures, art, and furniture—add a personal touch.

Simplicity shines when left to its own device, uncluttered and highlighted by contrasting paint.

It may seem like quite a menu, and certainly if you are planning a major overhaul, you will want to consult an architect or design specialist. Even if you are not ready to tackle the whole house—you would just like to work on the paint, for example, or get your landscaping under control—your best bet still may be to go to design professionals. For less money than you may imagine, they can create a coherent design plan that you can implement bit by bit.

If you would like to tackle the job on your own, begin by educating yourself about the architectural style of your house (for more on this, see page 30). Shapes, window styles, materials, textures, colors, accessories, and even plantings are well documented for all significant architectural styles, and design resources for the most common styles abound. Local architectural groups, historical societies, and home-design magazines

Details can make the difference, especially when grass-green shutters and bright copper roofing punch up a sunny yellow house.

can help you find ways to accentuate your home's innate style, which may have been lost or diminished by ill-planned "improvements." You could also try to locate your home's original blueprints. Often, a perfectly fine, well-designed house lies under decades of bad decision making by previous home owners and recapturing your house's personality is simply a matter of stripping away anything that was not the architect's original intent. The same is true of landscaping. It often is easier to clean the slate, so to speak—except for any old-growth trees—than improve your yard bit by bit.

Once you have a good sense of your home's style and elements, you can start to think a bit outside the box. Personal choices can add surprising freshness, fun, and interest to a house. Exposing yourself to others' design choices—by driving through your

The horizontal heavy-roofed mass of this house gains power and appeal with a trio of well-proportioned volumes.

Color—or the lack of it—can be striking when carried through into the landscaping, in this case, an abundance of exuberant iceberg roses.

neighborhood, looking through books and magazines, or watching television design programs—can provide inspiration.

You may want to break up a tall side of your clapboard house with sections of horizontal, then vertical, and then scalloped clapboard for a visual kick. You may plant mammoth sunflowers to tower next to your cottage entrance or plant a hedge of mauve hydrangeas along your slate-blue walls for a

beautiful spring display. You may replace expressionless windows with elaborate counterparts or streamline an overly fussy porch.

Finally, as you begin to implement your plan, be a rigorous critic. With each potential design option—whether it is a material, color, or planting—ask yourself this key question: How does this add to the whole? When all your choices work hand in hand, your home will be a joy to behold.

Personal choices can add surprising freshness, fun, and interest to a house.

Strong trim and accents, a subtly textured path, and well-manicured landscaping are the essence of this home's sense of orderly well-being.

A study in complements and contrasts, the linear nature of this not-so-common clapboard is softened by its curved fanlight and mounds of flowers lining the front path.

Minor Remodels

If a major remodel of your home's facade is neither in the budget nor, perhaps, even necessary, you may be quite surprised at how much bang for your buck you can get with smaller, more discrete remodeling projects. Here we look at some of the minor remodeling projects you may want to consider; you'll find more information about these and other projects in the Makeover Workbook that starts on page 102 of this book.

It's smart to have an overall plan and then isolate problem spots and prioritize which ones you want to solve first. Begin with a critical look at your house. Is your entry clear, inviting, and scaled to the rest of the house? Are your windows eye-catching? Does your foundation landscaping accentuate the architecture? Is your paint or siding attractive and in good shape?

A preponderance of home owners need to look no farther than the front entry or porch. In many cases, the steps, railings, posts, eaves, and lighting are meager, flimsy, or just plain ugly. They may look like, and probably were, tacked-on afterthoughts. Conversely, a solid, well-proportioned front porch—fully integrated into the structure and style of the house, well lit and with broad steps and a generous landing—can

BEFORE & AFTER
Completing a gabled entry initiated this series of small remodels, which included enclosing an open porch, painting the house and chimney a sweet blush pink, and planting a rollicking vine that runs along the roofline to smooth transition points of the structure.

totally change the facade of a house. Redoing the front entry rarely involves much structural work on the house itself and generally pays off in spades when it comes to resale value. A beautiful entry, perhaps with a porch broad enough to accommodate a bench or chair and some potted plants, is about as welcoming a sight as there is. For accomplishing this task, however, you will want to involve an architect or designer who understands how to blend the entry seamlessly with the architectural style of the house. Repainting the house and replanting the foundation border may be enough to make the remodel complete.

Nondescript, undersized front windows are another design flaw common to many homes. Windows, as they say, are your

BEFORE & AFTER These home owners spent little to create a big effect by replacing a spindly railing with wood, demolishing a planter to unleash a bountiful border, banishing an ugly downspout, and adding a decorative walkway and grass.

BEFORE & AFTER From messy to masterful: Adding a two-tier gabled entrance and brick porch gave grandeur to this otherwise undersized driveway entrance.

house's eyes on the world and one of the first things people notice, particularly if the windows are large, well-proportioned, and of interesting design. It is easier than ever today to find beautiful, energy-efficient windows to replace old, deficient ones. You can buy replacement windows designed to fit into existing frames, eliminating the need to tear into the house's structure.

If complete window replacement is not in the budget, you may consider dressing up the windows you have. One way is to add decorative wood framing to a frameless window, or a larger, more elaborate frame to a meagerly framed window. This type of improvement does not involve structural work and requires minimal repair to walls.

Another easy improvement is the addition of functional or decorative shutters. Shutters are available in many styles and can be dressed up with interesting hardware. Decorative iron grillwork also can add style where it is appropriate to the architecture, notably on Spanish- and Mediterranean-style houses, but make sure the grills can pop out easily in case of fire.

Window boxes are another inexpensive, lovely addition to front windows. (See more about window boxes on page 124.) Be sure to keep them beautifully planted and well watered. Adding pots of the same flowers to

BEFORE & AFTER A black umbrella awning, checkerboard landing, lattice panel, and new color scheme were easy additions with great visual impact.

BEFORE & AFTER With less than $200 worth of plants, these smart home owners turned bare-bones linear foundation landscaping into lush curves.

the front steps will integrate the effect.

You may even think of reworking existing landscaping as within the realm of a minor remodel. Certainly, a full-scale redo of the front yard can be a major expense, but if you want to take on your yard bit by bit, a good place to start is the foundation planting area. A generously sized, thoughtfully planted, lush border is an asset to any house. For this, you may want to involve a landscape architect, designer, or knowledgeable nursery person to help develop a game plan. The cost benefit here is that once the foundation planting is in place, you can use the same formula to develop other areas of the front yard, such as the border along the sidewalk.

Other cost-efficient ways of sprucing up a facade can include adding touches of texture. You may consider cloaking a chimney in stone or brick, covering concrete steps and landings with stone or terra-cotta pavers, and redoing the front pathway to match. You can also use different cuts of siding to create wonderful effects. Try breaking up the monotony of a horizontally shingled gable wall by replacing just the gable portion with scallop-edged boards in the same color or alternating a few rows of scalloped boards with vertical boards. You can also spice up a boring facade with some well-placed lattice panels, either freestanding or attached to the walls, but be sure to buy good-quality, sturdy panels, or have them custom made.

Sometimes, even minimal changes can go a long way. Install a new, well-crafted front door (see page 106), or give your old one a fresh face with a coat of paint and a new set of hardware (see page 110). When coupled with an interesting new light fixture overhead, these changes will give your house a real lift without breaking the bank.

BEFORE & AFTER
Sometimes renovating a porch means simply replacing lightweight posts and railings with a more imposing and appealing wood presence.

Modest Makeover

It often pays to rethink the front-yard function. These home owners made a savvy choice to carve a useful parking space out of superfluous lawn and service it with a handsome set of stone steps and effective landscaping. Broad front steps at the front door eliminate the need for the former nondescript iron railing, but iron makes a charming reappearance in a series of hayrack window boxes.

Sometimes good remodeling is a game of take-away. In this case, painted cedar shingles were stripped and sealed to show natural wood grain.

BEFORE & AFTER A major makeover of the facade made this house less forbidding and provided a place for guest parking and outdoor dining.

Do you want to completely modify your home's original architectural style, change its roofline, or alter one of its prominent design elements? Sometimes it takes more than a new lawn or a coat of paint to give your home the measure of curb appeal you want. To transform your house dramatically, it may take a major remodel. With an exterior overhaul, you can completely make over your home's appearance, boost its value, and gain benefits such as a more useable yard and increased natural light indoors.

While a surface improvement such as new siding can add texture to the outside of a house, a major remodel can actually change its profile. If your home looks flat and uninteresting from the street, adding a new architectural feature such as a portico, colonnade, or set of dormers can add depth. Installing new windows or enlarging existing ones can enhance a monotonous facade, particularly if your house can accommodate bay windows. Expanding an undersized stoop or a porch will improve your home's silhouette and add an aura of elegance. A major remodel makes it possible to bring style, visual interest, and character to a bland or ungainly structure.

Another spectacular way to change your home's appearance is to reshape the roofline. Changing the pitch of the roof will give a run-of-the-mill house more presence, and this improvement can completely transfigure

a structure with a low-slung mobile-home appearance. A higher roof also opens up design possibilities, allowing you to create bump-outs and step-backs. In addition, the extra height may make it possible to extend the roofline to tie in an addition or a porch. In the space beneath your new roof, you may gain attic storage and a place to run ductwork for heating and air conditioning.

The all-important entryway is another area where grand-scale renovation can make a big difference. Instead of simply sprucing up your old front entrance, consider creating a new one. Virtually any house with a flat-looking facade will be more impressive with an extended entry—whether that means a simple portico or an expansive front porch depends on your home's architectural style. A prominent, welcoming entryway will also make your home seem more hospitable. A trellis or a freestanding pergola can identify the entrance to your home and lead guests to the door. While you're at it, you can remake other crucial entryway components, such as the walkway, landscaping, and lighting.

Above: A terrace made from brickwork matched to the facade creates a seamless transition from the house to the reconfigured driveway. Plantings soften the hardscape and tie it to the lush greenery nearby.

Right: Details such as pilasters and a portico give the facade dimension and place the house within a definite architectural style. Formal landscaping reinforces the look.

BEFORE & AFTER A new front porch creates a prominent entryway for this house, which suffered from a fatal curb-appeal flaw: a hard-to-find front door. The porch's gables echo the angles of the roof and the new trapezoidal windows.

An ambitious exterior overhaul also provides you with the ideal opportunity to correct design flaws that keep your house from working the way you would like it to. You may want to relocate an awkwardly placed or hard-to-find front door, or reroute an intrusive driveway that is taking up too much of the front yard. If your garage is the first thing people see from the street, you may decide to convert it to living space or move it to the back of the house. If you want a place for outdoor entertaining or guest parking, include this area in your remodeling plans. A wide-ranging strategy allows you to tackle problems that might otherwise appear to be insoluble.

If your house is an architectural nonentity, a major remodel affords you the opportunity to give it an identifiable style. You can open up the front of a drab, boxy house with large banks of double-hung windows and add a portico, dormers, and pilasters for a classic Colonial look. A dreary 1950s ranch house can become a Southwestern hacienda with the addition of a Spanish tile roof, rounded windows, and a stucco finish. However, keep in mind that even a zealous remodel cannot change your home's basic bones. If you are renovating a single-story

BEFORE & AFTER A dominating garage and all-but-invisible entryway were the targets of this ranch remodel. Now, a courtyard (left) approaches the new front door, clearly identified by a pair of pillars. The garage became living space, and a new carport, flanked by matching pillars, now houses the cars (below).

A major remodel
demands vision,
effort, and a
generous budget.

BEFORE & AFTER
A Mediterranean-style tower
gives this ranch house a stylish
focal point. The colonnade
clearly identifies the front door
and underscores the
Mediterranean theme.

structure with a low-pitched roof, don't try
to give it the look of a Tudor.

Even if the outside of your house requires
no structural changes, it may need so many
cosmetic improvements that your budget no
longer befits a minor makeover. The good
news is that a project of such magnitude
invites you to address a variety of issues at
once. This approach makes for efficient
planning and construction and provides the
fastest route to a more beautiful house. It
also ensures that each aspect of your remodel is part of a harmonious whole. Should
your aspirations outstrip your budget, you
can still start with an imaginative and well-
considered master plan and complete the
project as time and money allow.

When you are considering an extensive exterior remodel, keep in mind that you are taking on a challenge. This caveat is even more important if creating an exterior look is part of a larger plan to expand your home's interior. In most cases, you will be required to obtain permits from your local building department before you can begin work, and you will need to pass inspections during each segment of the construction process. Because you'll face complicated design questions and perhaps structural issues, as well, it is best to hire an experienced architect. You will also need a general contractor who can supervise construction from start to finish. (For advice on choosing and working with a designer or architect and a contractor, see page 104.) To alter the roof or another major structural component, you may be obligated by law to bring in a structural engineer.

A major remodel demands vision, effort, and a generous budget, but there is no substitute for a bold, comprehensive approach when your house needs more than a little help to realize its full potential. A complete exterior makeover can increase the value of your property by 20 percent to 30 percent, but even more important is the satisfaction of living in a house that you are proud to call home.

BEFORE & AFTER When the interior of this home was re-oriented, so was the house's curb appeal. The old living room and stoop, which faced the street, were replaced with the double doors of a new master suite and a terrace.

A site-friendly home has a contour-hugging footprint and uses natural materials, earthy hues, and indigenous plants.

Where houses line up elbow to elbow, such as in a city or a citified suburb, the concept of a site-appropriate house is simple. A house that is site-appropriate has design integrity and fits within the style of the neighborhood. Furthermore, it often has plantings native to the area.

In regions where houses are fewer and farther between, where the natural world is much more conspicuous or even predominates, the concept of being site-friendly is a little more involved—though no less important to maintaining value and visual appeal.

The goal, as was said of renowned architect Frank Lloyd Wright's own home, is a house "not so much on the site as of it." Wright's philosophy of organic architecture—which often drew its shapes, colors, and materials from the actual building site—may be a bit heady when you are only in the market for boosting your home's curb appeal. But if your house is of a more generic style, you can borrow from the Wright sensibility to make significant changes to your home's appearance, resulting in a house that blends seamlessly with its environment.

Following are some ideas that can help you to create a truly site-friendly house:

Keep a natural color scheme. One of the least expensive, and easiest, ways to make your house more site-friendly is to take your exterior color cues from the site's environment. Wright picked his colors from the surrounding red cedars, white birches, and yellow-sand limestone where he designed. Earth tones visually minimize the shift from house to surroundings. They combine easily with each other for rich displays and generally are crowd pleasers.

Use local materials. Another Wright hallmark was to cull building materials from the site itself. Try to make use of regionally harvested wood for elements such as trim, siding, and even casual garden furnishings, and use locally quarried rock and stone pavers for pathways, planting beds, and stone walls. If your house is in a rocky area, think of installing some interesting boulders to serve as front-yard accents. In addition to being economical, boulders impart an immediate and unmistakable sense of place.

Maintain the site's topography. The less you disturb the natural flow of the land, the more the house will seem to be a natural part of the site. If the site and house style call for it, allow the entry pathway to wind like a stream to the front door. If you are building out a front-yard courtyard or terrace, work around or incorporate natural elements such as large trees, boulders, and outcroppings as much as possible.

Incorporate native plants. You will save yourself a lot of time, trouble, and money if you allow the natural landscape to guide your planting choices. Native plants look more suitable and perform far better than imports. Visually, they firmly place the house in its surroundings.

Echo vernacular architecture. Consider historical work buildings in the area—barns, grain silos, ranch houses, churches, and bell towers. If you are adding on to the house's structure, you may do well to incorporate these shapes in the design as a modern-day homage to local history. You also may want to make fresh use of old-style materials such as corrugated metal, tin roofing, or barn siding to enhance your home's connection to its place and past.

Below: A carefully planned take on nature, landscaping that mimics a dry creek bed allows a house to blend seamlessly with its surroundings. Bottom: The house keeps a low profile so the natural beauty of the site can dominate.

True to Form

The mixed pedigree of this Mediterranean house is celebrated through a variety of show-stopping details, including vivid white trim and hot citrus wall colors.

You want to spruce up your house's exterior, but where should you begin? If your house has a recognizable architectural style, perhaps you need not go any further than understanding, and being faithful to, the basic characteristics of that style.

Architectural styles come with a set of distinct design elements, often including colors and materials that can serve as a foolproof road map to a successful house rehab. With a little research, you can learn how to enhance your home by working within the vocabulary of its design, a process that often involves eliminating inappropriate add-ons. Enhancing your home's style also may command certain types of landscape details. If you do your homework, you will end up with a beautifully appointed, harmoniously composed exterior.

Architectural styles—and there are dozens—all have been well chronicled, analyzed, and dissected. A search of your local library, arts bookstore, or the architecture section of any good bookstore will yield books devoted to many of them. A broader search may include architectural and home-design magazines. The Internet is another good source for information on particular styles. If your house exemplifies a particular regional style, you can also look for a local architectural society that can provide a wealth of historic as well as practical information. All of these will be important resources, not only for inspiration but also for finding everything from specialty builders to products. Tag book pages and clip articles to compile an idea file that will serve as your renovation bible. When you are through, you will have learned a good deal about architectural history and will have an even greater appreciation and understanding of your house's pedigree.

Some of the most common architectural styles, and their characteristics, include:

Earthy yet elaborate, Mediterranean-style homes revel in sun-drenched details: wrought-iron gates, lighting, and hardware; exposed beams; tile roofs; stone and clay pavers; hand-crafted polychrome tilework; and rustic landscaping.

Mediterranean (Spanish or Italian) Revival

Popularized in the early part of the 20th century, this mixed style charmingly borrows elements from a host of Mediterranean cultures. While some examples are quite formal, others are much less so. What they have in common are a roughly plastered, light-colored surface, a low-pitched tile roof, smallish windows that are often arched and deeply cut into the facade, and a penchant for elaborate decorative ironwork on windows and elsewhere. Colorful, hand-formed Spanish or Mexican tile often is used to accent entryways and stairs; clay pavers or fieldstone are featured in walkways, terraces, and steps. Desert plantings set the proper mood, and roses and bougainvillea are also sometimes used to great effect.

The classical formality of the Greek Revival home is well demonstrated in this single-story version, a strongly rectilinear house with a low-pitched gable roof. The pronounced symmetry of the home's wide columned entry is emphasized by gabled volumes that flank the brick front steps. The front door and tall casement windows surrounding it are topped by transom lights, and other windows are punctuated by louvered shutters that occasionally butt up against the column capitals.

Greek Revival

A style popular in much of the 19th century, Greek Revival strove to re-create the feel of the classic Greek temples. This very formal design style involves large, simple structures encrusted with classical ornamentation, such as pedimented (or broken pedimented) gables, columned entries, cornices, and moldings. Tall windows are symmetrically placed on the facade. The preferred color is white, to echo the look of marble, but the trim is sometimes black. Symmetrically and formally placed manicured shrubbery complements the style.

Ranch

Ranch style, perfected and popularized by California architect Cliff May in the post–World War II period, has its genesis in the Spanish rancho as well as in Frank Lloyd Wright's Prairie style. Ranch design seeks to blend with the landscape, so informal landscaping of native plants, shrubs, and trees is the perfect complement. The single-story dwelling is notable for its broad, low-pitched wood-shingle roof and deep overhang; large bands of windows; wide chimney; and stucco, shingle, or clapboard sheathing. Earth tones are the preferred colors.

The ranch house's low profile, with its broad, low-pitched roof over a horizontal volume, allows it to blend well with the natural surroundings.

With its simple dignity, the Colonial house remains one of the most beloved architectural styles, and this example amply demonstrates why. Despite its rigid symmetrical design, temple-style portico entry, and heavy wood moldings, the Colonial never fails to offer a warm welcome, thanks largely to the cheerfulness of its multi-paned double-hung windows, paneled doors with sidelights and fanlights, clear-cut front path, and strong color.

Colonial Revival

If you have a true Colonial—that is, a house built during the Colonial Period, you likely already know it because you are living in a national treasure. More likely, you live in a house that is a contemporary version of the classic—Colonial Revival. Some of this style's features are a simple two- or three-story rectangular structure topped by a gabled or hipped roof; symmetrically placed double-hung, multilight, and shuttered windows; a centered doorway that is sometimes set with a portico and topped by a fanlight; classical detailing such as pediments, columns, and cornices; and brick or clapboard surfacing. Deep colors such as barn red, dark green, and blue work well, as do a number of landscape styles, from English country garden to a more formal look.

Saltbox

So named because its shape resembles that of a Colonial-era box used to store salt, the saltbox is similar to a Colonial in the symmetry of its facade and the use of double-hung windows. Because these houses originally were only one room deep, the sloping roof—longer on one side of the gable than the other—was developed to cover a single-story rear addition. Saltboxes, which generally are clapboard-clad, feature a prominent central chimney or a pair of chimneys at either end and a less elaborate facade than Colonials—for example, there is no portico entry. Saltbox houses take the same paint tones as Colonials, though often the wood siding is left to weather naturally. A landscape of wildflowers and other natural plantings provides the perfect rustic complement.

The extended side of the saltbox shed roof often masked an addition to the first or first and second stories of the original house, which typically was only one room deep.

At their best, Craftsman homes are paeans to the natural world and the art of hand-craftsmanship. The heaviness of the low-pitched roofs and front-porch constructions are meant to anchor the horizontal house shape to the site. Craftsman homes draw heavily on natural materials—wood, brick, and stone—and often on earthy hues for their color scheme.

Craftsman

This style is drawn from the Arts and Crafts movement, a philosophy based on closeness to nature and a respect for hand-craftsmanship. Its form was influenced by sources including Prairie style, the California bungalow, and the Japanese house. Its aesthetic rose to an architectural peak in Southern California. The style is distinctive, with simple box-like shapes under broad, low-pitched roofs hugging the natural contours of the site. Craftsman houses feature deep porches supported by massive square posts, pergolas, terraces, and screened sleeping porches to take advantage of California's healthful night air. Structures expose end beams and projecting rafters and often are clad in shingles or stucco, with wood left to weather naturally. Color schemes are often worked around earth tones. Informal gardens feature native plants, birds of paradise, and poppies. Pathways frequently are marked by a "rolled" concrete border.

Contemporary

An umbrella term used to refer to a number of modern constructions, contemporary houses tend to follow the modernist tradition of stripped-down, flat-roofed, mainly horizontal structures of various sizes and arrangements. The goals are to create a purity of line and diminish the separation of indoors and out through the use of large glass panels and glass walls. Contemporary structures often combine natural materials such as wood with either rough or stylized industrial materials such as metals, plastics, composites, and concrete. Landscaping of these houses is usually as stylized as the house itself, with simple, sculptural plant forms being the most successful.

Space-age sleek meets smart design for this contemporary home that abuts a busy boulevard. The architect kept the windows narrow and long on the public facade, opting for stem-to-stern glass walls for the side facing the private garden.

Color at Its Best

Color is one of a renovator's most powerful and versatile tools. Whatever exterior upgrades you choose to make, the colors you use—on your house and in the landscaping—will influence a first impression more than any other design element.

Color can be soothing, or it can sizzle. Exterior paint can provide eye-catching accents, drawing attention to architectural details. Similarly, landscaping can add spectacular shots of color that contrast with the exterior paint for added punch. Or, for a more subtle approach, you can choose both paint and landscaping from the same color palette to help your house blend seamlessly into its environment.

A good paint job, which can last 10 years or more, is almost always cost-effective—in fact, it is one of the best investments you can make for a home with an aging paint job. Not only will it protect the house's structural integrity, preventing moisture and the sun's ultraviolet

radiation from damaging siding and trim, but it will also make a house almost glow.

If you decide to have the job professionally done, be wary of a bargain-basement bid—a poor paint job will quickly fade, peel, and show cracks, leaving you with a house that, well, looks like it needs a paint job. Even though a high-quality professional paint job can be a significant expense, it's worth it in the long run.

If you decide to do the work yourself, be aware that it will entail more than a few weekends' worth of work. In fact, the prep work alone, which accounts for much more time than the actual painting, can take a month of Sundays. A thorough paint job requires that all loose paint be removed, cracks be opened and patched, and patching be allowed to dry completely. Wood trim should be sanded to the base, caulking should be scraped out and reapplied, and everything should be given a thorough priming plus two or three finish coats, preferably with a brush and not a sprayer.

It pays to know about the different compositions of oil/alkyd- and water-based latex

Taking a color cue from the giant allium in the front garden, this home's plum trim is well mated to the robin's egg–blue clapboard, and both are perfectly complemented by the rest of the front-yard flowers.

The fiery combination of taxi-cab yellow and burnt orange is allowed to dominate the front-yard landscaping of neutral-toned agaves and ground cover.

exterior paint on the market today. Though oil-based paint traditionally has been favored for wood, new latex paints are environmentally friendlier and can do a better job of holding color and expanding with the elements without cracking (see page 126).

In addition to the base paint, you will likely need another color for the trim and maybe a third for accents. Many paint companies understand that choosing colors can be very confusing and, because of this, offer color cards demonstrating tried-and-true paint

Above: Monochrome is anything but monotonous in the right setting. Right: Deep blue gets a jolt when a playful pop-out window is trimmed in bright yellow.

combinations, often tied to architectural styles, to help get you started.

Because painting is an investment, be generous with color sampling. A good way to start is to drive around and see what others have done. Don't be afraid to ring a doorbell or two to inquire about that perfect shade of burgundy on the trim. If you are preparing your house for sale, real estate agents will advise you to play it safe and go neutral, although a properly hued yellow house with white trim—the sunny cottage look—can also be extremely appealing. It can also pay, however, to be a touch offbeat. Cream with brown trim may be safely predictable, but what about cream with charcoal trim and khaki accents? Strive for a fresh take, but, above all, find colors that are right for the style of your house.

Don't be afraid to indulge your imagination—just realize you may have to experiment to get an unusual combination just right. That shade of Delft blue you crave may look charming on a 2-inch paint chip but may be

Because painting is an investment, be generous with color sampling.

Accentuating all of a Craftsman's positives is child's play when a complementary, multi-hued palette calls attention to the delightful details.

intolerable plastered across a 50-foot-wide facade. It may take a dozen samples to find just the right red for your front door. Paint will invariably look paler on a surface hit with sunlight than on the chip or in the can. When you see a color you like, you may want to buy quart samplers a few shades darker and lighter.

As you develop your paint color scheme, don't forget to consider the landscaping. You may want to choose colors that showcase your beautiful flowering spring trees or wisteria, or the amber and golden tones your trees turn in the fall.

Multicolor plantings often look their best against neutral backgrounds, while single flower and plant tones can be effective against stronger color schemes. Imagine, for example, banks of red roses against a cornflower-blue facade or borders of orange and yellow daylilies near deep-green walls. You may want to choose a flower color that echoes the hue of the trim.

Complicated architectural styles involving combinations of brick or stone with wood or stucco may benefit most from a quiet dark-green landscaping of manicured shrubs and trees, while rustic-toned Spanish-style houses are enriched by a desert's subdued palette.

With a little time and a lot of patience, you will be amazed at the rewards you will reap when you focus on color as a priority.

BEFORE & AFTER Different hues of the same color, highlighted by bright white, create high drama while effectively directing the eye to admire the details.

A Study in Contrast

When pondering color choices, think contrast as well as complement. Clockwise from upper left: The brilliant-blue window trim shouts out from the adobe-toned wall and is a foil for pink hollyhocks. There is no mistaking the entrance to this yard: The bright-red gate stands out amid neutral walls and green garden foliage. The soft beauty of salmon shutters perfectly complements the window box and border plants. Luscious lavender boldly outlines elaborate Queen Anne frippery and similarly toned impatiens.

Face Value

Sometimes it takes more than just a few coats of paint to make a house look the way you'd like. Perhaps the front of your home is flat and boring, or maybe it was "modernized" at some point and stripped of its original architectural identity. Maybe it's so worn-out that a simple touch-up won't suffice. In such cases, you can get dramatic results by making some changes to the facade.

The elements of the facade—features such as siding, roofing, doors, and windows—are so prominent that any one of them can determine whether your home looks appealing or appalling. The good news is that if all of these components are architecturally appropriate and in top condition, they can make even the most ordinary house look attractive and well cared for.

If the time has come to repair cracked siding or a worn-out roof, you have a perfect opportunity to make the face of your house more expressive. Instead of simply replacing what you have, consider options that will add character and texture. For instance, you can bring dimension to a bland box of a house by using shake-style roofing and highly decorative shingle siding. Keep in mind that it's best to hire a pro if you plan to replace large features such as siding and roofing.

Opposite: When arranged in a creative way, ordinary materials such as shingle siding and asphalt roofing can add plenty of texture to a home's facade.

An attractive facade remains true to a house's architectural style. Above: Traditional materials give the facade a timeless quality while preserving its contemporary look. Left: Wooden lap siding, double-hung windows, and neoclassical details enhance a Colonial design.

If your home's facade is in good shape, you may want to leave larger elements in place and concentrate on details such as exterior molding, shutters, and doors. A beautiful front door makes a house look both stylish and welcoming, and trimmings such as transoms and sidelights can increase the impact. Molding and other trimwork can turn a featureless house into a distinctive one, especially if you choose accessories that evoke a particular architectural era (for example, pilasters for a Georgian flavor or ornamental beams for a Craftsman look).

In most cases, the best makeover you can give your house is one that captures its original style; this approach is usually the most likely to increase the value of your property, as well. If your home has a definite architectural character, you'll simply need to make sure that any improvements to the facade will harmonize with what's already there. In the event that your house has no discernible style, remaking the facade will give you the chance to create one. Often the "bones" of your house will suggest a certain style; for instance, a structure with deep overhangs will readily accept Craftsman details, while a rectangular house with a centrally placed front door can take on a Colonial quality.

As you imagine a new face for your home, consider how it will look in the context of your neighborhood. You don't want to create a carbon copy of your neighbor's house, but

BEFORE & AFTER
A steeply pitched roofline and rustic shingle siding helped to tie in this home's new second story and enhance its cottage character.

The best makeover you can give your house is one that captures its original style.

it's also unwise to make your house look wildly out of place; in other words, think twice before installing vinyl siding if every structure in your vicinity is stuccoed. Above all, don't try to make your house into something it's not. A '50s ranch house will never become a gingerbread Victorian, no matter how much you rework the exterior.

If the cosmetic benefits aren't enough motivation, there are plenty of practical reasons to improve your home's facade. A shipshape facade protects your house from structural damage and gives it an aura of quality and solidity. It says that behind the pretty face is a home that's sound, secure, and weatherproof.

BEFORE & AFTER New siding and trim materials—cedar clapboards, beadboard, and diamond-shaped cedar shingles—along with an imaginative paint scheme gave this home new depth and interest. Adding porch columns and railings and replacing the small window above the gable also improved the house's overall proportions.

Window Treatments

When new windows are installed as part of an interior remodel, it's important to consider how they'll look from the outside. Windows come in a variety of styles; for maximum curb appeal, pick styles that harmonize with the architecture of the house. This new house gets a distinctive look with clusters of awning-style windows, triangular transoms, and elongated double-hung windows flanking a partially divided fixed window. For more about windows, see page 120.

W hen it comes to curb appeal, landscaping is as important an element as the house itself. A well-designed, well-kept landscape displays a house to its best advantage and conveys a message of conscientious care.

Few home improvements will give you a better return on your investment. The right landscaping can boost a home's value by 15 percent or more, and should you decide to move, attractive landscaping will help you to sell your house quickly. In addition, a skillful landscape design can simplify yard maintenance and can even reduce home energy bills.

An effective landscape blends with the style of your house, enhancing it without overwhelming it. It's designed to suit the conditions of both your yard and your lifestyle. It generally provides privacy while creating a welcoming atmosphere, and it reflects your personality. Above all, it makes it a pleasure to spend time outdoors.

Landscaping falls into two basic categories: formal garden design—which emphasizes order, symmetry, and geometric forms—and informal garden design, which uses flowing lines and diverse plantings to mimic nature. In many cases, your home's architecture will dictate the style of your landscape. A yard full of desert plants would be just right for a

BEFORE & AFTER A bald-looking facade becomes alluring when softened by grasses and climbing vines that create a feeling of intimacy and shelter.

BEFORE & AFTER A small box of a house gains country-cottage charm with the addition of a layered landscape that uses columnar trees and a vine-covered trellis to extend and define the entryway.

BEFORE & AFTER A house with an architectural identity crisis takes on a distinct Spanish personality when a formal lawn and boxwood hedges are removed to make way for a vivid Mediterranean garden.

Southwestern adobe house, but a stately Colonial would look better with clipped hedges and a neat lawn. Remember that the garden accessories you choose will also help you to define the style of your landscape. For example, terra-cotta pots with bougainvillea will evoke a Mediterranean atmosphere, while wooden trellises covered in climbing roses will suggest an English garden. It is also important to consider how the landscaping you have selected will blend in with your neighbors' yards.

The style of your landscape will have certain practical ramifications as well as aesthetic ones. If easy maintenance is one of your priorities, consider a minimalist design that makes generous use of mulching, ground covers, and hardscape features such as pathways. If you're planning to sell your house in the near future, you may want to stick with a conventional lawn and conservative plantings, which buyers often prefer to the wilder look of an informal landscape.

Once you've settled on a style, consider what you want your landscaping to achieve. You can use landscape elements to provide privacy, improve a view and even lower summer temperatures inside your house.

Trees, shrubs, and flowerbeds can serve the same functions as hardscape features such as walls, fences, and gates. Plants create natural

BEFORE & AFTER
Replacing a flat lawn with upright plants helps shorten the horizontal look of this low-lying ranch house, while a profusion of colors and textures in the garden adds interest to the facade.

You can use landscaping to camouflage unsightly areas of your yard or house.

boundaries and buffers, yet they have a neighborly, open look. When used to define your home's entryway or delineate the perimeter of your yard, they provide a feeling of enclosure and intimacy without presenting an unwelcoming barrier. On the other hand, greenscape elements can offer maximum privacy when you want it because plant heights aren't limited by local building codes. A living screen will cost much less than a fence or wall, and it will do a more effective job of controlling dust, noise, wind, and erosion.

Trees, shrubs, and even small plants create shade and absorb sunlight, cooling both your house and your yard. According to the U.S. Department of Energy, just a single strategically placed tree can save as much as 25 percent of a household's energy bill. Unless you live in a warm climate, consider deciduous trees and shrubs, which will block the summer sun and then shed their leaves in autumn to allow light in when cold weather arrives.

A successful land-

scape plan, like a well-composed painting, uses scale, form, color, and texture to create a unified, balanced whole. To make your landscape as interesting as possible, you will want to include a diverse mixture of trees and plants. Trees will bring a vertical dimension and a majestic quality to the landscape, while shrubs will define open spaces and create transitions. Perennials will supply depth and texture, annuals and bulbs will add seasonal color and fill in bare spots, and ground covers will provide continuity and give the yard a finished look.

You can also use landscaping to camouflage unsightly areas of your yard or house. You may want to grow vines across a chain-link fence or plant shrubs that will hide the garbage cans or the gas meter (but make sure the plants will not impede access). If your yard is small, you can make it look larger by planting trees and other tall landscape elements that direct the eye upward, much as a high ceiling creates a sense of volume in a small room. Or use bright colors in the foreground of your yard and pastels farther back to create an illusion of distance. To keep a long, narrow yard from looking like a corridor, position plants

BEFORE & AFTER Replacing the fence and trellis with a curving foundation garden full of big, colorful blooms better reflects the casual look of this cottage-style house.

The clean lines of succulents and grasses make a perfect foil
for a contemporary house. Below: Low-maintenance plants
with eye-catching shapes and textures add year-round
interest to this home's informal gardens and pathways.

Above: A gravel driveway has the enchanting look of a country road as it meanders through a woodsy, natural landscape. Right: Neat ground cover and low-clipped hedges serve a dual purpose, providing a soft outline for the driveway while drawing the eye toward the home's entrance.

Seasonal blooms add cheer to a run-of-the-mill asphalt driveway. A paver border keeps the look neat.

to divide the space into smaller areas that will break up the line of sight. If you have a driveway that is a formidable river of gray concrete or gravel, well-landscaped borders can dress it up—and at a fraction of the cost of a driveway replacement.

Before you select specific plants, consider what types will be the proper scale for your house and your yard. A large three-story home will look grand with towering trees and monumental shrubs, but the same will look awkward for a single-story ranch. If your house is low and rambling, stick with spreading shrubs, small ornamental trees, and other plantings that emphasize horizontal lines. If you have a postage-stamp yard, look for plants with smaller leaves and a more diminutive stature. Make sure that your plantings are in proportion to one another, as well. Foundation plantings, in particular, should step up to the house in layers, with tall plants at the back and shorter ones at the front. Keep in mind that tall plants will frame and accent, while low ones will invite the eye to travel.

Your next challenge will be to link these diverse elements visually. Choosing a definite style for your landscape will help. Once you have identified certain types of plants that evoke the style you want (for example, manicured hedges to anchor a formal design), you can repeat them throughout the landscape to create unity. Even an inconspicuous ground cover will accomplish this if you plant it in several places—around a tree, alongside a fence, and beneath a group of shrubs, for instance—so that it draws the eye from one element to the next. Using different plants with similar forms or leaf shapes will also have a unifying effect. Whether you like hot colors or cool ones, make your selections from the same palette to avoid a jarring effect.

As you're filling in your landscape, be sure to plan for the full-grown size of the plants

Plantings can dress up a driveway or path that's rudimentary or worn at a fraction of what it would cost to repair or replace hardscape elements.

For ultra-low maintenance, choose plants that suit the local climate, and nestle them close together to discourage weed growth.

you choose. Catalogs and guides list the heights plants will reach at maturity, as do the tags you'll find on plants at the nursery. And don't forget that different plants require different amounts of ground space; for example, one species of shrub will have a horizontal spread of 3 feet, while another type will spread to 8 feet when fully grown. When ground space is limited, look for "columnar" or "fastigiated" varieties, which will grow tall and narrow. You'll also need to find out when your plants will bloom, especially if you're trying to keep your yard colorful throughout the growing season. Keep in mind that vividly colored foliage, fruit, tree bark, and ornamental grasses can supplement seasonal blooms.

For long-term beauty and minimum upkeep, look for plants that will readily adapt to your climate. A plant that is ill-suited for its location will have a lackluster appearance

BEFORE & AFTER Drifts of hearty, low-growing bulbs, perennials, and shrubs spruce up a parking strip that was once a wasteland between street and sidewalk.

(if it manages to survive at all), and it will probably require a great deal of maintenance. Though plant adaptability is usually considered a function of cold tolerance, summer heat can also take a toll or cause damage. A local nursery or county cooperative extension office can help you find plants that perform well in your area. Varieties that are native to your region are the most likely to thrive.

Finally, consider the conditions in your yard. Plants have different sunlight and water requirements; to put them in the shade when they prefer sun (or vice versa) is to invite failure. Most plants are also rather particular about soil chemistry. A soil test, which can be done by a lab or with a do-it-yourself kit, will identify soil conditions that need to be amended. More than any other factor, the quality of your soil will determine how well your plants will fare. You'll be living with your landscape for years, so don't pass up the chance to give it a good start.

Tall plants such as sunflowers can create an airy privacy screen that encloses the house and welcomes guests.

Front-Yard Structures

Structures such as fences, gateways, and pergolas work together to anchor this house to its site and reinforce its Craftsman-like architectural style.

Does your front yard have good bones? The bones, or framework, of a front yard—structures such as fences, walls, gates, arbors, trellises, and pergolas—offer an effective means for giving the front of a house focal points, personality, and eye appeal.

For greatest effect, these structures should be designed as an integrated unit, echoing shapes and materials of the house's architectural style. Because of the complexities of creating a cohesive design, employing a landscape architect or designer to draw up plans is often a good strategy. In addition, you may want to hire professionals for some of the construction work, but some projects, such as installing trelliswork or building an arbor, are good weekend tasks for a person with moderate carpentry experience. Structures available as pre-cut kits, ready to be assembled on site, make the work even easier.

As you begin the design process, you may want to start with the perimeter—the fencing and walls. Because fences and walls likely will be the largest front-yard structures, their design can have significant impact. Both walls and fences establish boundaries, but they can do much more. Think about what other functions you want them to serve. For

example, do you want them to create a safe zone for young children or pets? Do you want more privacy? Your answers to such questions will help you to determine the best types of walls or fences for your front yard.

Walls make a formidable perimeter. Masonry walls look great with certain types of homes—especially formal architectural styles. A stucco house, for example, will look best with stucco garden walls that are the same color as the house.

Though you may want to install one wall around the front yard, a single wall isn't the only way to go. For example, you can layer walls to create front planters. If your house sits above street grade, you may want to break down a mountain of lawn with a series of low walls flanking the entry. If privacy is your goal, you may indulge in a wall as high as local

A freestanding white wood pergola, accented with a red mailbox and pots of geraniums, casually but firmly establishes the entry to this home.

Fences do more than mark territorial boundaries—they set the tone for the property. Those that utilize well-crafted lattice panels are particularly neighborhood-friendly and also let light penetrate to border plantings. Above: Lattice panels are paired with solid fencing. Top right: Full lattice panels are inset between brick columns. Right: Ornate posts and gracefully curving rails create a classic feel.

building codes will allow. If you do, consider piercing the wall with openings or softening it with plantings to avoid the "fortress" look. Generally, for the property to remain street-friendly, the house facade and front door should be visible over or through the wall.

Fencing is, for the most part, less permanent, less imposing, and less expensive than a masonry wall. Most fencing is made of wood or metal, and materials are commonly available at most home centers for do-it-yourselfers. However, if you have the budget for it, consider a custom fence that will set your home apart. A house with arched windows will sing behind a similarly arched fence design. Split-rail fencing enhances rustic-style homes, and a woven metal fence will stand out in front of a modern house.

Alternate materials, such as bamboo or rice paper—like fiberglass paneling are also worth considering. Combinations of materials can be interesting, as well—imagine inexpensive pine fencing set between brick or stone posts.

Fencing doesn't have to be solid. A common fencing system involves solid planks

Rambling plantings soften
the hard edges of this
softly weathered fence,
which features a mix of
solid and lattice panels.

Pergolas can be used to create a sense of entry, as evidenced by this iconic garden gateway set in stone and flanked by lattice panels.

topped by trelliswork or even trellis panels set between posts. Fencing works well with most architectural styles, but as a rule, the more formal the house, the more substantial and formal the fence style should be.

If money is limited, you may consider opting for inexpensive fencing and expressing your personal style through a signature gate. Made from wood, metal, or a combination of materials, gates range from humble knee- or

waist-high styles to commanding portals in single or double styles, depending on the size of the entry pathway. Some gates incorporate arbor trellises, mailboxes, and even small tête-à-tête benches for quick chats with passing neighbors. Gates can be forbidding, but the most pleasing allow at least a glimpse of the property beyond.

Walls, fences, and gates are common front-yard fare, but some of the more unusual and fanciful designs come from trelliswork, arbors, and pergolas.

Trellises—latticework of thin, lightweight crossbars usually set in vertical panels—are garden workhorses. They can attach easily to facades to support tall plants and vines that add a visual kick. They can be installed atop fences or be set into or made into fences. A humdrum garage front gains instant appeal from simple trelliswork framing the door. An unsightly wall can be beautifully camouflaged with trelliswork. Prefabricated panels, often of redwood but also of high-density polyethylene are easily obtained at local home centers and lumberyards.

Arbors are metal or wood structures, sometimes curved across the top, that often are designed to support tall-growing plants such as vines or climbing roses. Arbors incorporating a gate make a fine floral or leafy entry. Consider punctuating a pathway with a series of rose-covered arbors or stationing a pair on either side of the house as entries to the side yards. A favorite, and

This archway adds depth and definition to the simple front fence entrance.

charming, cottage element is a vine-covered arbor surrounding the front door.

A pergola, from the Latin word for "projection," resembles an arbor in its purpose to support plantings, but it generally frames a walkway. The most common pergolas are done in classical style, as was the fashion in ancient Rome, and feature round columns with pedestals. Another beautiful style is the square-post Craftsman pergola with distinctive notched and angle-cut rafters.

Classical pergolas usually are painted marble-white, while Craftsman styles are either stained or left to weather naturally. All pergolas feature sturdy support posts topped with heavy beams. These beams are crossed by rafters crowned with narrow bars, or "purlins." A pergola generally needs to extend logically from one place to another. It makes a fine entryway from the street to the front door, for example, or from the door to the front-yard terrace. If you have tall fencing surrounding your perimeter, you may attach a pergola to the inside wall and create built-in bench seating for quiet contemplation or intimate conversation.

In this modernist setting, precision drilling creates a thousand points of light in otherwise sternly opaque metal gates.

Heavenly Gates

Gates are most often the focal point of front-yard structures such as fencing and are great opportunities for style and personal statement. Wood and iron—or a combination of both—are the most common materials. The best are custom-made, but some fine specimens are available through home improvement centers, online vendors, and a multitude of catalogs. While perimeter gates generally focus on the front entry, try offsetting a gate to direct visitors' gaze to an intriguing landscape beyond.

Inviting Entries

A home's entry is its welcoming handshake, inviting guests in from the street or driveway and along walkways, steps, and landings to the front door. The elements that constitute the entry should work as a seamless unit to ensure safe and interesting passage from the public domain of the street to your private world. Because the entry is the first taste your guests will have of your home, it deserves every bit as much attention as any room in the house.

As you begin to assess your entry, look at the established route. Some houses take the no-nonsense approach—straight as an arrow from the sidewalk to the front door. This scheme works very well, particularly for highly symmetrical and formal styles of architecture such as Colonial, Georgian, and Greek Revival. The straight walkway should be announced with a bit of fanfare through the use of substantial pavers or paver groups. And to complete the effect, symmetrical landscaping should border the path from one end to the other.

Asymmetrical architectural styles, in which different-sized volumes combine and

BEFORE & AFTER A cottage entry gains texture, structure, and personality when rustic rock walls, steps, and a walk-way replace a nondescript front lawn.

the front door is usually offset, benefit from a meandering walkway. This is particularly true of cottage-style homes, ranches, and rustic Spanish or Mexican haciendas or any other house that has a casual, humble profile.

The wandering path can be a voyage of exploration for visitors if you make the most of this opportunity to please and surprise guests. Create pools of interesting plantings, perhaps accented with a fountain or other garden ornament. Wind the path around a wonderful old tree or a large boulder, or past a particularly lovely window.

If your front yard is perfectly flat, you may consider having a landscaper sculpt some

BEFORE & AFTER Removing stark railings gave this front entry room to blossom with a charming profusion of potted plants.

A winding river of brick marks a clear and sweetly meandering path through grass and deep borders to this home's front door.

A front path should accentuate a house's architecture. A symmetrical brick house, right, is well served by its formal brick walk, but a country home, below, can take a more casual approach.

low berms that add a bit of mystery to the approach. A curving pathway has an added bonus—it makes a short front yard seem much larger. Paving materials can be more casual, as well. Flat stone, broken concrete, and even wood rounds set in ground cover make wonderful choices for this approach, but be sure to make the steppingstones generous in size and maintain them scrupulously from overgrowth, or the trip could become somewhat hazardous.

If your home requires steps to the front door, consider creating those steps from the same paving materials used for the pathway or from complementary materials. The idea is to create a seamless entry.

Next, look at the front door's surroundings. If your house has a landing, strongly consider paving it with the same materials used in the pathway. Keep in mind that a landing also gives you an opportunity to

Stone pavers set in a pool of grass, an irregular stone stepway and landing, and a curved stone wall add both structure and spirit to this humble cottage.

welcome guests. Consider incorporating a design pattern—inset tile or a circle of stone or brick, for example—to symbolize the journey's end and announce "you have arrived." If the landing does not already have some sort of covering—a pergola, portico, or trellis—to create a sheltered way station before entry, consider adding one to bring texture and volume to the facade.

The front door, in addition to its obvious function, has tremendous symbolic value. When people look at a house from the street, instinctively, they look for the front door. The more accessible and friendlier it appears, the more inclined they are to be

drawn to the house. A simple, inexpensive paint job can do wonders for a nondescript door. Try a bright color, a shade different from the house's wall and trim paint, and you will have a door that is eye-catching.

Invest in high-grade door hardware—a solid, heavy doorknob speaks volumes. Install an interesting, sculptural door knocker, even if you have a bell or intercom entry. For an added sense of welcome, install fixed glass panels and fanlights in the wall area next to and above the doorway. In addition to bringing natural light into your house, these windows give a peek into the home and a taste of what lies beyond the threshold.

A stairway need not just be a stairway. Above: A series of steps and landings allows visitors the opportunity to stop and smell the roses. Right: A cascading fountain takes its shape from the adjacent brick stairway.

The Door to Success

Because the front door is the reward at the path's end, anticipation is everything. Set the scene any number of intriguing ways. Frame the doorway in an interesting manner, and dress it up with decorative paint or wood treatments. Or use rustic posts and beams or evocative columns to buttress the entry. Put in lively plantings to soften the edges, richly textured pavers to cloak the steps and landings, and lighting that makes a statement. The only limit: Be true to the house's architecture so the entry is an asset, not a liability.

Lighting the way

The best way to make an entry inviting at night is to light it thoughtfully and carefully. Though motion-sensing floodlights would provide you with security, nothing could be less aesthetically appealing. If you light your front property well, you will not need such security lighting.

Pathways should feature staggered lighting that clearly illuminates the walk's parameters. Uplighting trees and large shrubs will lend dramatic effect. Any steps should be very well lit across the treads, onto the landing, and up to the door. And, of course, no inviting entry is complete without a good lighting fixture. Depending on the style of your architecture, a sculptural fixed light or hanging lantern can make for a beautiful focal point.

An entry can be dark and forbidding without an investment in proper outdoor lighting. Above: Lights ingeniously set into fence posts subtly, but clearly demarcate the property. Right: Uplights at the base of trees and path lights combine to lead the way through this enchanting front-yard forest.

Proper front-yard lighting may include a number of different types of fixtures, as shown below.

Spotlights highlight trees, large bushes, and shrubs.

Canlights suspended from limbs provide illumination from above to highlight a sculpted tree's natural beauty.

Decorative copper lights help delineate and showcase flower beds adjacent to the pathway.

Driveways & Garages

A driveway is a great opportunity to add texture to the front yard, as evidenced by this engaging assembly of stone blocks in a variety of sizes.

Often one of the biggest missed opportunities in maximizing a house's curb appeal is the "car zone." Few home owners manage to integrate the driveway and garage area into their overall design, and, as a result, this area is left a functional, but lifeless no man's land of dull hardscaping. Fortunately, thanks to new methods, materials, and ideas, much needed attention is being brought to this "lost" area of property. Without a great deal of money, it is possible to recapture this space in a stylish, value-enhancing way.

Driveways, those gray rivers of poured concrete, have undergone a renaissance in recent years. The look of pricey stone pavers, brick, and cobblestone, once the province of estates and high-end homes, is turning up more and more in middle-class neighborhoods because structurally sound faux versions of these materials have entered the market at cheaper price points.

The point-counterpoint design of this smooth concrete driveway and checkerboard-paver carport area makes a pleasing marriage of function and form.

Using the same material for the driveway and the pathway to the house creates a unified design.

A center strip of contrasting material, stone, or plants can break the monotony of a broad swath of driveway.

BEFORE & AFTER A circular drive carved into a super-fluous front lawn creates a gracious entry.

The best news may be new technologies involving concrete. Today, concrete's signature gray can be given different looks, including tints and textures. For more about the many options available to you, see page 178.

The driveway's layout can also make a difference. One of the easiest and cheapest methods of dressing up a long concrete drive is to cut a central canal down the middle and plant grass or ground cover in it or fill it with gravel or stones.

Keep in mind that driveway construction involves heavy-duty, skilled work and the results are virtually permanent. It is best left to a professional.

Another increasingly popular driveway improvement, particularly for families with young children and an otherwise enclosed property, is a driveway gate. Gates can be manually operated or motorized and made of wood or metal. If you are adding a driveway gate, be sure to pick a style that complements your architecture—no Spanish baroque filigree wrought iron for a Tudor or a Colonial house, for example.

BEFORE & AFTER The addition of a brick and iron fence adds structure to the vast no man's land of this home's driveway, creating a carport and a more formal entry for visitors. Brick columns and detailing inset in the driveway complement the home's exterior.

One Sea Street

A well-designed gate set either at the front (shown here) or rear of the driveway (shown below) encloses the property while adding to the landscape.

There are three basic types of gates: single swing, which opens either to the left or right; bi-parting, with two panels that open from the middle like French doors; and sliding. Swinging gates tend to be less expensive and easier to install than bi-parting ones, but you will need at least 12 feet of level space on either side of the gate. Manufacturers recommend a single swing for a driveway 14 feet wide or less and a bi-parting style for a driveway more than 14 feet wide. If your driveway ascends steeply or you get a great deal of snow in the winter, you will need to choose a slider.

The most convenient gate openers are automatic. There are hand-held remotes that can be used from the car, keypads that function with punch-in codes, and intercoms and telephone entries that dial up the house. Exit sensors—either push-button, keypad, or underground—automatically open the gate for exiting. If you opt for an automatic system, be sure to have a photo eye installed that will reopen the gate if it hits an obstacle.

Garages, once lowly outbuildings, are becoming design elements in their own right. As a rule, garages, even if detached, should pick up elements of the house's architecture. For example, if your house has a shingle roof, so should the garage. If your garage is something of a blank slate, try installing windows, decorative wood details, or hardware pieces that match those featured on your house.

Garages that are attached to a house are already part of the architectural scheme but often do well with a bit of embellishment. Trelliswork or an attached pergola outlining the garage door is an inexpensive way to dress up a garage front.

Generally, a garage's main design element is its massive door, so the right garage door can make a tremendous impact on a home's curb appeal. For more information on garage doors, see page 182.

Gorgeous Garage Door Design

If your garage door presents a large, foreboding image when viewed from the street, seize the opportunity for eye-catching design. Some new doors are made from technologically innovative materials that are superbly functional as well as beautiful. Garage doors should complement and never compete with the design of the house. You can make a design statement with the addition of pergolas, window inserts, extended eaves or awnings, bold hardware, and interesting lighting fixtures.

Decorative Details

Sometimes it is the little extras that can elevate a lovely house, with the exterior right and the garden in sync, into something truly special. Think of it as set dressing, or setting the scene. These personal touches make the mood, express your family's personality, and welcome your guests with an intimate touch.

Start with one of the most basic, and most overlooked, functional elements—your address, or, more specifically, your house numbers. Often treated as an afterthought, house numbers are usually small and tacked up where they can least be seen, ending up behind an overgrown foundation shrub or tree. If you consider your house numbers as a true design element, new worlds open up. A trip to a hardware purveyor or a stroll on the Internet will quickly demonstrate just how many interesting and unusual options there are. They come in an enormous variety of typefaces and materials, including cast aluminum, bronze, brass, iron, stainless steel, ceramic or ceramic tiles, and imitation stone. If your street is particularly dark, consider

Playing the numbers game—house numbers, that is—is a great way to add fun to a functional element.

This home's natural charm is enhanced by such details as the gable's expert half-timbering, window boxes, and distinctive shelving for potted plants.

Left, bottom left, and below: Whether handcrafted or store-bought, window boxes, when well-planted and maintained, add color, texture, and great appeal to any style of facade.

A leafy iron bench, complete with wrought-iron wreath, evocatively offers respite.

The investment in movable plants is small but can make an amazing difference.

Basic clapboard gets dressed up with fan-top posts, frilly hanging planters, and a flash of lacy wood trim along the roofline.

reflective numbers or numbers that light up from behind. Whatever type you choose, make sure the font and materials suit the architecture of your house and the numbers are large enough to be seen clearly by someone walking along the sidewalk or driving down the street.

Planters, urns, and window boxes can make spectacular design statements. They add liveliness and color to dark or dull spots; help mark entry points, steps, and landings; and generally serve as eye-catching accents. Not all need to be floral. Compact, neatly trimmed hedge plants or topiaries make wonderful urn choices for formal houses. Planters and window boxes can bring life to windows and walls, especially if they contain colors that either pick up an exterior paint color or contrast well with the trim—think pink against a blue exterior, orange against green or another earth tone, or red against white or cream.

The investment in movable plants is small but can make an amazing difference. There are a few rules well worth considering. While you can use a variety of pots, make sure they harmonize in texture. In other words, don't mix terra-cotta with enamel pots. Second, keep the plantings well-watered and fresh, and replant often if you use annuals. Do not let plants start to die, and do not let them grow out of control, or your house will simply look unkempt.

Another design element that can add much to your overall design is your choice of garden furniture. A beautiful cast-iron or wood bench, chair, or glider is a wise addition to most front yards and porches. If you have the tree limbs to support it, a well-built swing holds great charm. These furnishings provide visual focal points as well as comfortable places to perch and watch the world go by.

In the right spot, decorative paint work such as a mural or stenciled border can be quite effective. If you have a covered doorway, the wall adjacent to the front door can be a prime spot for a vista mural that opens

Painterly touches can enliven a front yard. Clockwise from above: The classic Romanesque archway surrounding the doorway is totally faux, as is the door's classic finish. Mosaic artistry transforms a walkway into a serene blue pool topped by floating leaves. The delicacy of this wrought-iron tree-of-life gateway perfectly counterpoints the heavy stone-wall surround.

the space visually. Tile and mosaic likewise can be used to great effect, either in creating murals, as accent borders, or on staircase treads or pathways to the front door.

Tile tends to work best in Spanish- or Mediterranean-style houses, and the more rustic and authentic the tiles are, the more evocative the look. Mediterranean houses also do well with wrought-iron detailing such as handrails, railings, and door and window grillwork, although many Southern-style homes also can be embellished with finely done, often painted, grillwork. If you choose to install grillwork, make sure the style of the grill works well with the house's architecture, and—most important of all—

be certain that all grillwork covering windows can easily pop open for quick escape in case of fire.

One of the most distinctive ways to put a personal mark on your front yard is through garden art. Garden ornamentation can range from simple windmills and freestanding trellises to birdbaths, sundials, English mirror balls, and mobiles. Other options include imposing fine-art sculptures and statues in stone, metal, or wood. The subject of garden art is tricky because it reflects so completely the taste of the owner, which may or may not be the taste of the beholder. It helps to use a light hand and not overwhelm the space—a little art can go a long way.

Finishing Touches

The interplay of shapes can add layers of complexity to even the simplest front yards. The decidedly tropical house below is a lively mix of verticals—corrugated roofing and fencing—and horizontals—the roof vent, louvered shutters, and siding—broken only by the curvy waves on the front gate. Fencing is a great opportunity to get your design point across, whether with copper-topped posts, incised railings, classical references, or hardware that echoes the shape of the slats.

BEFORE & AFTER Porches that appear to be afterthoughts benefit when they are enlarged and integrated into the design of the house.

A gracious porch can add immeasurably to the charm of a house. Porches, after all, are one of the most enduring images of Americana. They hearken back to an era when family and friends would gather on wicker chairs and porch swings to relax and greet neighbors on warm summer evenings.

If your house already has a front or wraparound porch, be sure it's putting its best foot forward. Inspect it for any damage, especially for leaky flashing, a roof in disrepair, or clogged gutters and downspouts. And, if its paint has seen better days, give it a fresh coat or two.

You can also enliven an existing porch with architectural embellishments such as corner brackets or interesting trim. Large hanging baskets of flowers centered in the porch openings

can brighten the look (keep them well watered) and so can vines or roses creeping up trelliswork at the corners. Because your porch furniture is on view, keep it freshly painted and the upholstery clean and in good shape to make the space welcoming.

If your house doesn't have a porch, don't count yourself out. Most styles of houses will accommodate the addition of a porch — the key is to match the porch's materials and primary features, including roofing, to those of the house. For its architectural style, a porch relies most heavily on highly visible elements such as posts and railing systems. Posts or columns can be set singly or in pairs or threes at the corners. They can be smooth or grooved and cylindrical or tapered at the top. They may be made from wood, brick, stone, stucco, or other masonry construction or of a metal such as steel. Wood railings come in many shapes, and balusters can be square, round, or flat with cutouts. Ironwork, too, can be done in any of a variety of patterns and designs.

BEFORE & AFTER A standard two-story clapboard takes a grand turn with the addition of a graciously columned front porch that stretches across the width of the house.

BEFORE & AFTER This too-shallow porch was extended to not only make the space usable but also add a touch of elegance to the facade.

BEFORE & AFTER The addition of a deep front porch with accompanying stepped rooflines adds layers of design depth to a plain-Jane facade.

BEFORE & AFTER Breaking the roofline and reorienting the front steps gives this porch integrity and personality.

Porch floors are generally wood plank, concrete, or tile, and ceilings are wood bead-board or stucco. Wood is the most common porch building material; cypress is a popular species because of its weather resistance and ability to hold stain or paint well. Some ornate porches take advantage of molded polymer (composite) millwork that mimics the look of wood but resists insects and rot.

If you wish to add a porch—and your house, lot, and local codes will allow it—plan to make it at least 6 feet deep (from front to back) for comfortable seating. If you can extend out 8 to 10 feet, you will be able to make a true outdoor room that will accommodate a small dining table, small lounge chairs and couches, and perhaps a swing. The length and width of the porch should be in proportion to the house—if the porch is too large, the house will be overwhelmed, and if it's too small, the house will look silly. Because the style must blend seamlessly with the existing architecture, you should strongly consider consulting an architect or designer; this is nearly always worth the investment.

For the greatest flexibility of use, be sure to install good overhead lighting and electrical outlets. If your front yard does not get adequate breezes and you live in the Sunbelt, you may want to include ceiling fans. You can also consider roll-up screens or outdoor drapery to cut hot spots during the day. Just keep in mind that all of these elements will be visible from the street and so should be chosen for form as well as function.

A screened porch, while highly practical and very comfortable, doesn't have as much curb appeal as does an open porch. However, in parts of the country where bugs can present a serious problem, screening is a necessary evil. Consider installing removable screen panels with very fine, dark screening that virtually disappear from view. To minimize the negative impact on the look of the porch, make the panels the same size as the porch openings.

BEFORE & AFTER A wraparound front porch, with a built-in capital clearly marking the front entry, unifies the hodgepodge elements of this facade.

Secluded Surprises

You might not guess it from the street, but beyond this home's gated entry is a gracious entertainment patio, complete with an outdoor fireplace and built-in seating.

While many home owners like having their front yards and house facades clearly visible from the street, others prefer to create a bit more separation from public view and, as a result, have the opportunity to carve out a private outdoor "room" in the front yard.

This strategy can make sense both practically and financially, particularly if the house's square footage is tight. It often doesn't take much space to create a highly useable open-air front-yard patio, courtyard, dining, or entertainment area. Done properly, this can give a literal breath of fresh air to a home's design and add considerably to a house's value. The trick, of course, is doing it right.

The idea of a front-yard entertaining space is hardly new. Spanish, Mediterranean, and European designs—archetypes of a good deal of American architecture—have long incorporated beautifully landscaped courtyards, often punctuated with a small fountain, as pass-throughs to the home's actual entry. These versions usually were thick-walled and behind elaborate gates that gave mere glimpses of what lay beyond. Of course, such courtyards were not exactly "neighborhood friendly." The downside of tall, opaque, unadorned walls or fencing and heavy gating is that they can look defensive, secretive, and even a bit scary from the street.

The design challenge in creating a front-yard structured space is threefold: to enhance the house's architecture; to achieve privacy without alienating the neighborhood; and to maintain a clear path to the home's front door.

Any permanent structure needs to blend with or complement the house's overall architectural style. A Spanish- or Mexican-style

Stepped and fenestrated walls and low fencing combine to keep the patio private but not forbidding.

BEFORE & AFTER Sacrificing a scrap of lawn, these home owners created a cozy stucco and lattice front-yard getaway, complete with a bubbling fountain to welcome visitors as they enter through the new arched portico.

courtyard with a rustic fountain, no matter how much you crave it, will never look right with architecture of a different style. Similarly, if your house features clapboard or shingle siding, a stucco wall will look out of place. Be sure to choose materials that match your home's exterior. As you design the enclosure, also try to incorporate elements from the house itself—the same hardware or lighting fixtures or the same millwork detailing, for example.

One of the best ways to keep a front-yard structure appealing is to landscape it generously. Plant a beautiful border along the base of the walls. Let tumbling vines, rambling roses, or sprays of bougainvillea colorfully soften blank walls. Allow patio landscaping to creep up and over the wall to break down the separation of spaces.

You can also create appeal by punctuating walls with small "windows," perhaps echoing the house's window shapes. These can be set high enough to maintain privacy while presenting a welcoming face to the street.

BEFORE & AFTER Extending the white stucco walls and red tile rooflines added a natural slope that embraces this new front courtyard, which can be viewed through the massive grid gate.

A colorful profusion of potted plants and quaint tiles (below) marks and celebrates the entry to this home, where a tile-adorned courtyard fountain and an equally lush container garden await.

Fencing can be similarly opened up or topped with open latticework. You may not want to build walls at all—a "green" wall can be lovely to look at, if you have the patience for it to grow in. Good lighting can also keep a structure from seeming fortress-like. Uplights along the wall base and lighting at the corners define and demystify the structure.

With another "room" in the front yard, the pathway to the front door can become lost or confused. If the structure takes up only part of the front yard, and the front door lies outside the structure, make sure to clarify the walkway to the door. Doing this may mean installing a bolder series of steppingstones or broader steps. Large pots of plants stationed on either side of the door also work well to identify the entry. Be sure to light the way clearly. If the front door lies within the structure, so that the front gate to

the courtyard is the de facto front door for visitors, try to keep it friendly. Consider installing a window grille to give a view to what lies beyond.

With these points in mind, it can be exciting to start thinking about the possibilities for developing your own front-yard room. Even the smallest patch can be structured and organized as a quiet reading nook or a place to hang a hammock. Larger spaces offer even more options: dining areas, grill islands, bar areas, fire pits, or fireplaces. And property need not be level. Charming outdoor terraces, on one or more levels, can be tucked nicely off stairways leading to the front door. You will want to consider carefully the placement of the room in relation to its use. For example, if you intend to cook and dine in this front-yard space, access to it should be from the kitchen, dining, or family-room areas—not from the living room. If you see your terrace as simply a social place to have a drink and talk, living-room access is appropriate. A play yard should be accessed from the family room or kitchen, and not from the living room, unless you are happy to scrape sand and mud from your living-room carpet on a daily basis.

As to the design of the area, the sky is the limit. Be sure to light the space well for after-hours enjoyment. Built-in seating along the walls can keep furniture needs to a minimum. Consider installing a water fountain or wall cascade. Front yards are almost certainly noisier than backyards, and nothing blocks street noise more pleasingly—or muffles private conversations more thoroughly—than the sound of trickling water.

This beautifully rendered iron gate (shown above) allows a glimpse of this patio's inner life, which includes a welcoming stone fireplace.

Flights of Fancy

One home owner's salute to suburbia—a fragment of the iconic white picket fence, complete with mailbox, elbows aside the front path to take center stage.

A hidden surprise, a fun use of common materials, a twist on the expected—touches of whimsy can bring a smile to visitors and add a delightful dimension that makes a house one of the friendliest homes on the block.

Fencing is a natural foil. One of the easiest ways to add interest is to replace the tried-and-true ball or acorn finials on the post tops, particularly those flanking the front gate, with something amusing—a fanciful birdhouse, perhaps, an unusual lantern, or even a tipping watering can that appears ready to give a dousing to birds or passers-by.

Fencing itself can rise above the commonplace, yet still serve its function, just by an interesting choice of materials. Imagine, for example, a "floral" fence made of slightly bent, crisscrossing rebar poles topped with soldered metal flower cutouts. The effect is that of an airy flower border, made substantial by the use of rebar, an inexpensive building material. Fiberglass paneling, often used as transparent patio roofing material, has evolved from the wavy style of the '50s; some panels today have the delicacy of rice screens more commonly used indoors and can add an Asian or Zen touch.

You can also create a living fence around your front yard or along the driveway with certain types of trees (such as apple or pear) trained in the espalier method. A common European practice for centuries, this is a technique of pruning and bending major branches to grow in a flat plane against a fence, wall, or trellis. Trained to grow to a given height and supported by lightweight posts and wires, trees take on a solidity after a few years that rivals any fence material, but the effect is about as charming as it comes. And, as the trees go through their blossoming and fruiting cycles, the effect changes with the seasons. Young espaliers can be

Above: The lock-step lineup of this fence's pickets is matched by a row of uniform, shoulder-to-shoulder boulders.

The fencing of this curved flower garden does double duty by incorporating a pair of charming birdhouses in the entry posts.

Touches of whimsy can bring a smile to visitors and make a house one of the friendliest on the block.

ordered these days through fine nurseries and are well worth the investment for the years of delight they can provide.

Pathways are another prime spot for interesting touches. You may want to create your own concrete steppingstones fashioned with colored rocks or shells gathered on family trips, children's drawings or handprints (or the family dog's or cat's pawprints), imprints of leaves from your trees, messages or pictures drawn into the wet cement with sticks, inset tile, and so on. These efforts not only personalize your property but also provide you with lasting memories.

Hidden surprises are also fun elements. Tuck any type of stone or cement animal to peek out from under a bush, or hide it in a hanging basket by the front door. Birdhouses, particularly those done as art

pieces, can be interesting sources of fun garden ornamentation.

Another beloved, and often fun, decorating element can be the weathervane. A rising sun, a clipper ship at full sail, a sleepy owl—weathervanes have historically been a source of art and whimsy. Often crafted in copper to weather beautifully, weathervanes can top a roof cupola or sit on a pedestal or post in the front yard for show. They come in just about any design you can imagine, or you can have your own custom designed and crafted.

The common mailbox can also become uncommon when it appears in distinctive and amusing shapes. Sharks, barns, buses, and boats—just as with birdhouses, many mailboxes today have achieved the status of art pieces. You can even have one designed to look like your house.

Above: Rustic just doesn't get more charming, as this home's guard duck can tell you. Right: Sitting atop a tall column, this "marlin manse" echoes the house's design.

The unexpected makes for a surprising delight. Left: Hayrack window planters offer a cornucopia of fruit. Below: Thirsty visitors can sip from a porch-post fountain.

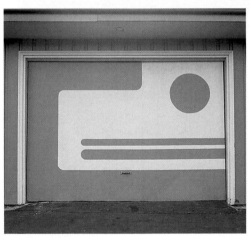

A two-tone retro twist elevates the common garage door to artistic heights.

Giving your yard character may be as easy as adding a personality such as this sleepy gardener, crafted from terra-cotta pots.

Makeover Workbook

Now that you've had a chance to browse through scores of great ideas and focus on what you would like to do to give your home more curb appeal, how can you make these dreams a reality? This chapter will help you accomplish your goals.

It begins with a discussion about how to work with professionals, helping you to streamline the process of finding good help and avoid the pitfalls and problems that can occur. Then it moves on to a detailed look at the specific elements you will likely be dealing with in the various projects you undertake. You will find information to help you choose products and materials—including front doors, roofing, siding, windows, paint, and garage doors—that can make a big difference in how your house looks and functions. And to help you update front-yard elements, the chapter offers a detailed look at materials and techniques for improving your yard's landscaping and hardscaping, from lawns and ground covers to fences, driveways, and water features.

Doing some or all of your own work is a great way to save money, engage in the creative process, and enjoy the satisfaction of accomplishment.

Throughout this chapter, illustrated step-by-step projects offer guidance for curb-appeal improvements that are within the skill sets of most do-it-yourselfers. Refinishing a door, building a lattice porch skirt, making a window box, painting trim, building a fence, planting a lawn, installing a new walkway, building an arbor—these are just a few of the projects you will find.

Whether you intend to do your own work or bring in professionals, this chapter will be a helpful reference and a hands-on guide to getting the job done right.

Working With Professionals

Major grading and construction—or any jobs requiring heavy equipment—are best left in the hands of professionals.

In many cases a bit of elbow grease and a few basic do-it-yourself skills are enough to enhance a home's curb appeal. Some jobs, however, require the kind of time and expertise that only a professional can provide. You may want an expert to help you with part of your project, or you may want someone to handle it from start to finish. In either case, it is important to find capable, reputable pros whose qualifications match your remodeling goals.

If you are planning to make extensive changes to the outside of your house, an architect can create a design that is aesthetically pleasing and structurally sound. Architects are licensed by the state and are qualified to make calculations for any structural modifications that may be needed. They can also oversee every phase of a remodel, from hiring a general contractor to supervising the actual work. Some architects charge a percentage of the total project cost, while others charge hourly rates.

A general contractor is the person who can bring your design to life. Licensed by the state to handle all aspects of construction, general contractors usually schedule and supervise subcontractors, such as electricians and carpenters—although some general contractors do all the work themselves. You will save 10 percent to 15 percent of your project cost by acting as your own general contractor, but remember that you will have to supervise workers, order materials, keep detailed records, learn about building codes, and provide insurance.

When you are replacing one of your home's major exterior components, consider hiring a subcontractor who specializes in a particular area of construction. Many large-scale exterior projects pose safety risks or require special skills that are beyond the abilities of the average do-it-yourselfer. Roofing and siding are among the tasks that should generally be left to experts who are familiar with the material you are installing—especially because improper installation can shorten product life and void warranties.

If your property needs a complete front-yard makeover, you may want to have a landscape architect draw up plans. Landscape architects are qualified to design and develop every aspect of the outdoor environment, and their input can be indispensable if your yard requires a complicated feature such as an intricate drainage system or a hillside terrace. You will pay about half the cost of a landscape architect for the planning services of a landscape designer who understands garden design and knows the plants that thrive in your area. A landscape contractor can handle all facets of installation, including excavation, grading, planting, and constructing hardscape elements such as patios and water features. If your property has a steep slope or unstable soil, your local building department may require you to have a soils engineer sign off on your project.

Before hiring any kind of expert help, interview several candidates who have been recommended to you by a reliable source, such as a friend or a professional you have worked with before. Ask all the candidates you are considering to provide references, and speak with their former clients to find out whether work was completed on time and within budget. Whenever possible, visit job sites in person to examine work firsthand. Make sure to verify credentials; contractors and architects should be licensed, and contractors and subcontractors should be bonded. State boards, professional societies, and organizations such as the Better Business Bureau can tell you whether any complaints have been lodged against the person you are thinking of hiring.

When comparing costs, ask every professional for a written bid that includes price breakdowns for all materials and labor. Be sure that you understand what each candidate's bid includes; a low-priced contractor may be using cheaper supplies or less-meticulous construction methods. If you will be expected to pay on a time-and-materials basis, ask for an estimate with a "not-to-exceed" figure. Do not make a final decision on the basis of cost alone. In the end, you will

save money by hiring someone who gets the job done right and completes it on time. A professional's availability may also be a factor, especially if you live in an area where winter weather can make exterior remodeling impossible. Above all, pay attention to your gut reaction. It's important to find someone you can work with amicably.

Once you have chosen a professional, get a written contract, and read it carefully. Make sure that any agreement you sign spells out exactly what you expect, including start and finish dates, specific job and materials descriptions, the professional's responsibility in case of accident or theft, warranties on workmanship and materials, and a payment schedule. Do not agree to make a final payment (usually 10 percent of the total) until the job has passed final inspection and is completed to your satisfaction. Depending upon where you live, you may also need to include a "waiver of subcontractor liens," which will prevent suppliers from putting a claim on your property if the general contractor fails to pay for materials used on your project. Keep a copy of your contract on file, and make sure both parties initial any changes that are made to the document along the way.

Site visits by members of your professional team—such as a builder and an architect—are critical to working out details.

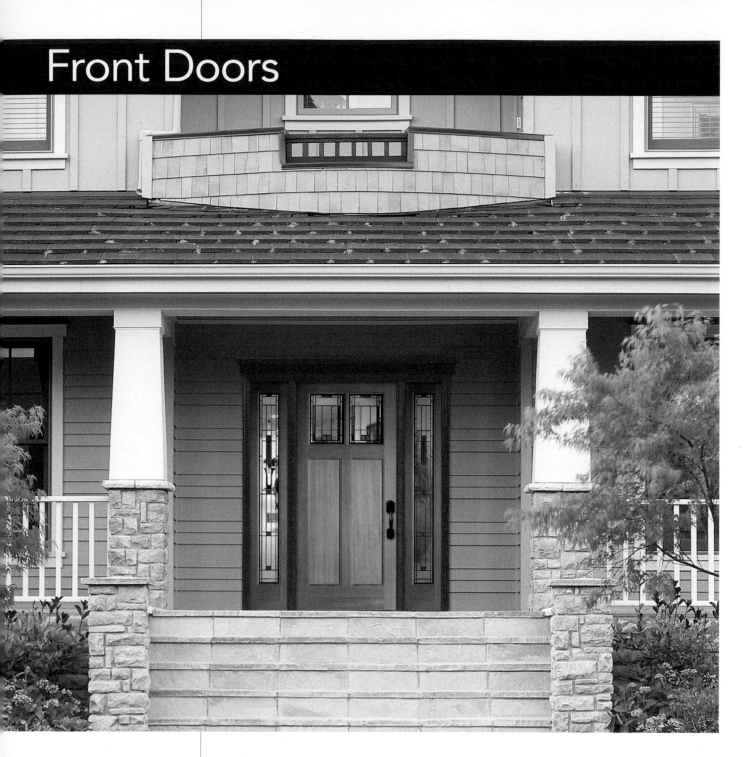

This beautiful natural-wood Craftsman-style door with dual sidelights in leaded glass is just the right touch for a stately home.

When it comes to first impressions, the front door is a key focal point. It is the first part of the house that guests see closely and, as a result, it sets the tone for the rest of the house. Ideally, it should emphasize your home's style and character.

But entry doors often show their age prematurely because of weather and wear. Most older front doors are made from wood, which is warm and natural but vulnerable to the elements. Eventually, a wood door tends to warp and crack. See page 110 for ways to give an aging wood door a facelift.

If your front door is beyond repair or you're ready to step up to a more beautiful, efficient entry door, a better option is to replace it. Hundreds of types are available, from conventional wood models to steel and fiberglass-composite entry systems.

Door Construction

A door is specified as either "flush" or "paneled," terms that define the door's method of construction or, in the case of doors that are not made of wood, the door's general style and appearance.

Paneled doors have rectangular recesses, or "panels," framed by horizontal rails and vertical stiles. All-wood doors made this way have superior strength, and this type of construction minimizes cracking and warping because the panels have room to shift as they expand and contract with changes in temperature and humidity. Because the look is more traditional than that of flush doors, many nonwood doors are given the appearance of this construction.

Flush doors are flat and smooth on both faces. Wood flush doors are covered with a wood veneer that is easy to stain and varnish or paint. Nonwood flush doors are clad with fiberglass or steel. They may have a solid-wood or insulation foam–filled core.

All swinging doors are attached to the jambs with two or three hinges. On exterior doors, the hinges are on the inside of the house to prevent removal of the hinge pins by an intruder.

Glass sections of doors are called "lights," and the pattern of the lights is identified by their number. A six-light door, for example, has six glass panes, separated by muntins (wooden dividers). You can buy true divided-light doors, or, if you just want the look of divided lights, you can buy snap-in muntins or between-the-glass muntins that mimic the look but are a less expensive option and make the glass easier to clean.

Standard doors are 6 feet 8 inches tall, but you can buy doors up to 8 feet tall. Widths of exterior doors range from 30 to 36 inches; a wide entry door will make it easier to move furniture into and out of the house and provide for wheelchair access. Door thickness is typically 1¾ inches.

You can buy an entry door singly—as a door meant to be mounted in an existing frame—or pre-hung in a frame. A pre-hung door usually comes as a complete entry system, with an integral interlocking threshold and weather stripping encircling the door's perimeter. With an entry system, sidelights may flank the door and a transom window may cap the top. Because hinges and the lock set are designed as part of the system, these doors tend to be very weather-tight and extremely reliable.

Door Materials

While most doors are made from wood, an increasing number of today's doors are manufactured from other materials. The face materials are often wood, fiberglass composite, and steel. The core or interior structure may have a steel or wood frame, and many exterior doors have foam insulation filling the voids between the framework.

Wood Wood has the warm, natural look and feel that most people prefer. But because

An entry is at its best when it is designed to reflect the home's architectural style.

wood will eventually warp, crack, and bow when exposed to the elements, it must be maintained with a durable finish. Solid-wood doors tend to be more expensive than doors made from other materials. Species include oak, cherry, walnut, mahogany, maple, fir, pine, or paint-grade doors from any of several softwoods.

Most mass-produced "wood" doors are not solid wood. Instead, they are made with an engineered-wood core that is faced with a veneer, a construction that minimizes warping and movement and makes the doors inexpensive to build. Be aware that veneers are easily damaged, particularly if they are thinner than about ⅟16 inch.

Fiberglass composite Where a door will be exposed to weather or particularly harsh or humid climates, fiberglass-composite doors are a smart choice. These doors realistically imitate the look of wood, thanks to a combination of molded wood-grain texturing and a wood-like cellulose coating that can be stained. A fiberglass door's framework is usually made of wooden stiles and rails and filled with a core of foam insulation.

Fiberglass doors, like wood doors, are sold as single units or as complete entry systems with appearance-grade wood jambs, a variety of glazings, adjustable oak sills, and security strike plates. Many fiberglass door entry systems are guaranteed for as long as you own the house.

Steel Steel doors are extremely rugged and durable. Although some steel doors have traditional panel styling, they are not true panel doors—they have a steel or wood frame and are filled with foam insulation.

Most steel doors have surfaces of heavy-gauge galvanized steel. Conventional steel doors are factory-primed with a baked-on polyester finish. Some are given a vinyl coating for greater weather resistance. If you

Above: Wood is the standard by which other doors are measured. This classic is accented by a full-height leaded-glass sidelight.

A stained wood-grain surface helps this fiberglass door convincingly imitate hardwood.

want the look of wood, you can opt for a steel door that has been embossed with a wood-grain pattern or, better still, you can choose a type that has been given a wood-fiber coating or a real-wood veneer that can be stained.

Custom Doors

If you'd like a front door that is truly unique, check out specialty-door companies that design and create custom doors. You can find such companies listed under "Doors" or "Millwork" in your phone book, or you can search for custom doors on the Internet. Most companies offer specialty doors that can be made to fit your home, or they will design and build doors from scratch. The majority of custom doors are made from hardwoods; some incorporate stained glass or other specialty glazing and have arched or elliptical tops. Expect a 4- to 16-week turn-around time after ordering.

Above: A steel entry door with decorative glass offers both style and high durability.

This custom door and its sidelights are a honeycomb of wood and glass.

BEFORE & AFTER

New brass hardware—including door knocker, numbers, kick plate, and latch—gives this door an entirely updated look.

Buying Tips

When replacing an existing door, measure the width, height, and thickness of the actual door. When buying a pre-hung door, measure the width of the existing jamb, from the inside of the exterior molding to the inside of the interior molding. Note which side the knob is on from inside the room. If the knob is on the right, the door is a "right-hand" door; if the knob is on the left, it is a "left-hand" door.

When buying an entry system, make sure all of the door and jamb components are from the same manufacturer—not products assembled from different distributors—to ensure they will work together effectively.

Updating a Front Door

If your front door looks weathered, shabby, or just plain boring, you may be able to give it a new lease on life by refinishing it or updating it with new hardware.

Refinishing a door is a relatively simple project because a door is a small, flat surface that is easy to work on. Plan to work during nice weather, when you can leave the door open, but do not work in direct sun or overly hot weather. It is usually easiest to leave the door on its hinges and protect the floor and area around it with drop cloths. But if the hinges are caked with paint, you may want to remove the door and replace the hinges or drop the hinges in a bucket of paint stripper to remove the paint and then buff them.

As shown in the steps below, refinishing a door involves removing the lock set and surface hardware, stripping or scraping off any flaking paint, sanding the surface, priming the bare wood, and then repainting.

For best results, apply two coats of a slow-drying alkyd/oil primer; topcoats of both alkyd/oil-based and latex paints are compatible with this type of primer. Fill any cracks or gouges with vinyl spackling compound after priming the door. For the topcoat, choose a high-quality gloss or semigloss 100 percent acrylic latex paint. (See more about paint on page 126.)

Brush in the direction of the wood grain. For a panel door, first paint the panel moldings, the panels, the horizontal rails, and then the vertical stiles. If the door is flat, you can use a fine enamel roller to apply the paint and then stroke the paint in with a brush, using vertical strokes and brushing toward the middle.

New hardware can make a dramatic difference in the look of a door. Lock sets, kick plates, doorknockers, house numbers—all of these come in many styles and finishes from home improvement centers and hardware supply stores. House numbers, kick plates, and doorknockers are simply screwed in place. The complexity of installing a new lock set depends upon the style—all new ones come with complete instructions. Just be sure to buy a lock set that will fit the holes in your door.

Refinishing a Door

1 To remove the door's lock set, first remove the interior plate and knob; the latch bolt in the edge of the door; and then the exterior trim, latch, and cylinder assembly. If removing the lock set looks like it will be too much work, simply protect it with masking tape.

2 Sand the surface by hand, beginning with medium sandpaper and graduating to fine grit. Sand in the direction of the wood grain. Feather (smoothly blend) the transitions between previous coats of paint.

3 Prime any bare wood using a trim brush to apply two coats of alkyd/oil primer, allowing the first coat to dry before applying the second. Fill any cracks or holes with spackling compound after priming. Finally, apply one or two finish coats of 100 percent acrylic latex paint.

Siding & Roofing

Though this home's walls appear to be clad with classic board siding—appropriate for the architecture—they're convincingly covered with more durable vinyl siding.

No elements have more impact on the overall look of a house than the roofing and siding. These two components cover most of the house's exterior surface and set the tone, style, and character of the house. Because of this, your home's curb appeal depends largely upon these elements being in top form.

When roofing and siding are in poor shape, they make a house look shoddy, and, even worse, they make it susceptible to weather damage. You can do simple siding repairs yourself (see page 114), but for most roof repairs, it is best to call a roofer. On page 117, you will find information on cleaning siding. For information on painting, see page 126.

It may make sense to completely re-roof or re-side your home, particularly if you're doing other major improvements. As part of an exterior design scheme, roofing and siding must be more than attractive—they must be architecturally appropriate. When choosing siding and roofing materials, the key is to look for beautiful, durable products that harmonize with the style of your house. To help you make decisions about the best types of siding and roofing for your home, the following information offers a look at key options.

Buying Siding

Siding comes in a wide array of styles and materials. The type that is right for your home depends on your house's architecture, your budget, and the amount of maintenance you are willing to do.

For beauty and versatility, nothing beats wood siding. Typically made from cedar (although you can also get pine, spruce, redwood, cypress, and Douglas fir), wood siding is available in boards, shingles, or shakes.

Wood Wood lap siding, made of overlapping horizontal clapboards, is characteristic of classic American architectural styles such as Colonial and Craftsman, and it is still a top choice among designers of upper-end houses. Board-and-batten siding, a less common style in which boards are installed vertically, is more suited to contemporary designs. Shingle siding, typical of country-cottage and Victorian styles, comes in a variety of configurations for maximum design flexibility and decorative flair. Wood shakes have a rustic look. Though unmatched as a design element, wood requires vigilant maintenance: It must be sealed on both sides before installation and resealed every few years to prevent deterioration. It is also expensive, and high-quality products can be difficult to obtain. If you are considering solid-wood siding, enlist an experienced architect or contractor so you get what you pay for.

Composite Composite-wood products are less expensive than solid wood. Plywood siding is the least costly and the easiest to install. Often used in lower-end construction, its performance can be disappointing, especially in harsh climates, where moisture can cause plywood panels to delaminate. (Pre-priming panel edges and caulking seams will help.) Oriented strand board (OSB) and hardboard products are sold as 4-by-8-foot sheets or are molded to look like clapboard.

Although hardboard sidings failed on thousands of homes in the '80s and '90s, siding manufacturers have taken steps to improve their products by adding preservatives, additional primers, and adhesives.

Vinyl The most popular wood-siding substitute is vinyl. Available in both shingle and lap styles, vinyl is much less expensive than wood, but in appearance, it is no substitute for the real thing. For many people, vinyl's major attraction is reduced maintenance—it never needs painting, and because it is colored all the way through, it will not show nicks and scratches. It does, however, need to be cleaned regularly, and it can be damaged by impact, severe wind, and extreme temperatures. For maximum durability and realism, be sure to buy a top-quality product. An experienced contractor is crucial because even the most expensive vinyl siding will buckle and warp if installed incorrectly.

Fiber-cement (sometimes called "cementious") siding is another wood look-alike that is sold as planks, panels, and shingles. It will not rot, burn, or attract insects, and

Below: Plywood siding rides the curves of this contemporary house. Panels of plywood install quickly and cover with minimal seams.

Solid-wood siding is right at home on a traditional house. It can be painted or stained to enhance its natural beauty.

Above: Stucco siding suits this Spanish-style home. Above right: Wood-shingle siding, divided-light windows, and a porch create a cottage look.

it inhibits fungus growth. Fiber-cement siding, like wood, requires regular topcoat maintenance, but manufacturers claim that it can hold paint five times longer than wood. Fiber-cement siding costs about half as much as cedar, and the top brands carry a 50-year warranty.

Aluminum Aluminum and steel siding are fireproof, affordable, and, in most cases, easy to install over existing siding. Styles include lap, shingle, and board-and-batten, and many manufacturers offer matching trim. Color choices, however, are limited, and

metal siding is prone to denting. In all but the mildest climates, steel siding is preferable to aluminum, which is too soft to weather natural hazards such as hail and high winds (although aluminum may be the better choice if you live in an area where salty ocean breezes or air pollution cause steel to corrode). An experienced installer is a must if you choose steel because newly cut ends will rust if not protected from the elements.

Stucco Stucco continues to be a popular siding material, particularly for use in Southwestern, Mediterranean, and contemporary architecture. Once considered a high-maintenance exterior finish, stucco is now formulated with epoxy, making it simpler to clean and less prone to cracking. Traditional stucco is applied by hand and can be tinted to produce a surface that will not need to be painted. Chips and cracks can be repaired by a skilled do-it-yourselfer.

Simple Siding Repairs

If your home's siding problems are nothing beyond a few split boards, you can usually fix them by gluing and nailing or screwing the siding pieces together. But for more extensive damage, it is easier to replace boards or sections with matching pieces. Because most problems are caused by water damage, it is important to find and fix the source so it does not occur again.

When replacing damaged lap-siding boards, work from the bottom up.

For wood siding, cut the damaged section at each end and then lengthwise using a circular saw with a blade depth set just shy of the siding thickness. Pull or cut off any nails that were used to attach that section. Then trim a replacement board to the same length, and tap it into position (for tongue-and-groove siding, you will need to cut off the backside of the groove). Nail it in place, and caulk the seams.

To replace a section of vinyl or aluminum siding, use a utility knife or tin snips to cut vertically at both ends of the damaged section and horizontally across its center, and then pull out the siding. Cut a replacement piece 6 inches longer than the damaged section, and cut the nailing strip off of the replacement. Apply a bead of polyurethane caulk or lap seal to the damaged panel. Press the replacement section in place so each end overlaps the existing siding by 3 inches. Hold or prop up the new siding until the seal is dry.

To patch a hole in stucco, remove loose stucco with a cold chisel and ball-peen hammer; blow out the dust. Paint around the edges of the patch with a concrete bonding agent. Staple new wire mesh over any damaged mesh. Spray the area with water, and apply stucco repair mix according to the manufacturer's directions.

So-called "synthetic stucco," technically known as exterior insulation and finishing system (EIFS), consists of flexible panels covered with an acrylic coating that mimics the appearance of plaster. EIFS has been plagued by moisture-related problems, but manufacturers now offer products with "water-management systems." Proper installation is essential to avoid water damage.

Stucco siding, whether synthetic or traditional, is relatively inexpensive—about 20 percent less than cedar clapboard for a hand-applied finish.

Brick and stone Brick and stone are handsome, timeless siding materials that complement most architectural styles. Exceptionally resistant to pests, fire, and impact, brick and stone require little maintenance—although the mortar used at joints needs to be restored, or "tuck-pointed," from time to time. Because of their high cost, masonry materials are often used to provide a decorative accent for less expensive sidings. For about half the price, manufactured stone offers a similar look and easier installation. It comes in a wide variety of shapes and colors and is light enough to be installed directly over many types of existing siding.

Buying Roofing

Keep in mind that roofing is a major exterior design component, particularly if the roofline is steep. When choosing a roofing material, make sure that its color, texture, and composition are compatible with the style of your house. Unless the roof is a dominant architectural element, stick with muted colors that will not overpower adjacent siding. Keep in mind practical considerations, such as the fact that a light-colored roof reflects sunlight, and be certain that the material you pick is suitable for the pitch of your roof (a flat or nearly flat roof requires a seamless covering). Buy the best you can afford to protect your

home and maintain its curb appeal for years to come.

Asphalt-shingle roofing is the most popular type, thanks to its price and adaptability. It comes in an enormous variety of styles, colors, shapes, and textures, making it compatible with any architectural style. Quality varies, depending on how the shingles are constructed. Those with fiberglass cores may last 20 years; extra-thick fiberglass/asphalt-laminate shingles, known as "dimensional" or "architectural" shingles, often carry longer warranties. Inexpensive felt-core shingles, which typically carry only a 15-year guarantee, may not be permitted by local codes.

In many cases, new asphalt shingles can be installed over existing ones. Check with your local building department to see how many layers of asphalt roofing are allowed.

Wood shingles Cedar shingles and shakes have a distinctive natural look that suits many types of architectural styles and siding materials. Shingles and shakes are available in various grades and have 30- to 50-year

Top: Asphalt shingles are the most affordable—and often most sensible—roofing choice.
Above: Wood shingles are favored for their natural look and, on this home, provide a handsome backdrop for white-trimmed windows.

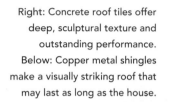

Right: Concrete roof tiles offer deep, sculptural texture and outstanding performance. Below: Copper metal shingles make a visually striking roof that may last as long as the house.

less than convincing. Painted finishes and high-tech coatings come in a variety of colors to match any exterior. Standing-seam metal roofing, the most common type, is suitable for a low-pitched roof and has a sleek appearance that complements a contemporary home. A steel standing-seam roof will last from 25 to 30 years.

Clay and slate For a historic or high-end home, a clay tile or slate roof offers incomparable beauty, elegance, and durability. Clay tile, which lends authenticity and charm to a Mediterranean-style house, is renowned for its ability to withstand extreme conditions such as fire, earthquakes, and heavy winds. Slate shingles are as indestructible as they are beautiful, often lasting for hundreds of years.

These masonry materials are heavy—up to three times the weight of asphalt shingles. Some roofing systems cannot support such a load, so be sure to have your roof evaluated by a qualified professional who can tell you whether your house will need structural reinforcement. Even without extra installation expense, slate and tile will have a big impact on the bottom line.

guarantees. Top-quality shakes made from straight-grained wood are expensive compared with economy shakes. (Lower-cost sawn shingles with thinner butt ends are best reserved for use as siding.) For an additional cost, shakes can be treated with preservatives and fire retardants. Shakes should not be used on a roof with a vertical rise that is less than 4 inches per horizontal foot.

Metal Metal roofing is exceptionally lightweight, strong, and resistant to wind and fire damage. It is manufactured to mimic a range of materials, including asphalt shingles, clay tiles, shakes, and slate, but imitations can be

Concrete tile Concrete-tile roofing—which is molded to resemble clay tile, slate, or wood shakes—offers a range of decorative options with excellent durability. Concrete tiles are lighter than clay or slate and require no extra structural support. The cost of concrete tile is similar to that of cedar shakes.

When figuring the cost of new roofing, be aware that the price depends upon your house's configuration as well as the price of materials. A steep roof—or one that includes gables, dormers, chimneys, or skylights—will require extra installation time. A large roof with simple lines may cost less to cover with roofing than a small one with a complicated design.

Cleaning Siding

Sometimes when a house's siding looks like it needs a coat of paint, all it really needs is a good cleaning. If your home's siding is looking a bit dingy or dirty, a logical first step is to clean it. Cleaning is also an important preliminary step to painting to ensure proper paint adhesion.

Before washing siding, cover plants, stone and brick walls, and patios near the house with plastic tarps.

Use a broom to sweep off loose dirt, working from top to bottom. Next, hose down the walls, and, if necessary, brush them with a stiff-bristle scrub brush and a solution of trisodium phosphate (TSP) or a nonphosphate substitute. To mix the solution, follow the directions on the label. Because this solution is caustic, do not use it on bare wood.

Brick or stone may suffer from efflorescence, a white powdery deposit caused by mineral salts that are dissolved by water and then appear on the masonry surface. First, brush and scrub as much of the deposit away as possible without water, and then follow with a thorough hosing. In an extreme case, use a 1:9 acid-water solution on concrete or dark brick and a 1:18 solution on light brick. Because muriatic acid may slightly change the color of any masonry, be prepared to treat the whole area to ensure an even color.

You can retard the growth of mildew by washing siding with a solution of ⅓ cup detergent, ⅔ cup TSP, and 1 quart household bleach in 3 gallons of water. Brush this solution onto the walls, and then rinse it off.

When working with muriatic acid or bleach, pour the acid or bleach into the water when mixing—never the reverse. Wear old clothes, eye protection or a face shield, and rubber gloves, and follow all label directions. Wet the surface, and then apply the acid solution with a stiff brush to one small area at a time. Let the solution stand for 3 to 4 minutes, and flush with water.

Pressure Washing Siding

One way to make quick work of a housecleaning project is to buy or rent a power washer. Power washers—high-pressure cleaning tools—are particularly useful for large jobs or for extremely dirty surfaces. Such washers force water through a handheld nozzle, allowing you to blast away dirt (and loose paint, so be careful). Most models have a separate reservoir for cleaning agents, enabling you to use the same tool for cleaning and rinsing. Be sure to read the operator's manual before using a power washer.

When using a pressure washer, follow these rules: Do not try to remove paint from wood or brick—when held in one place, the strong spray will erode wood grain and mortar. Do not use it on hardboard siding because water will penetrate and damage it.

Pressure washers are rated according to the pounds per square inch (psi) of pressure they deliver. For materials such as wood, aluminum, and steel, a 1,200 to 1,500 psi model is best. You can use a stronger 2,500 to 3,000 psi model if you want to work more quickly.

After filling the washer with the cleaning solution recommended by the manufacturer, hold the nozzle about 24 inches from the surface, squeeze the trigger, and slowly spray back and forth, adjusting your distance from the wall for the most effective cleaning. Work in 5- or 6-foot sections. When cleaning wood, be careful not to force water under the boards or to erode the grain. Wash the gutters and fascia, then the eaves, and then the walls. After using the washing solution, rinse the area thoroughly with fresh water (you can also use a garden hose for this step). If you intend to paint after washing the house, allow the area to dry for two days.

When washing a house, work from the top down.

Project: Building a Lattice Skirt

Removable lattice panels conceal the structure beneath this front porch.

If your home has a raised front porch, one of the best ways to spruce it up—and make a dramatic difference in your home's overall curb appeal—is to skirt the area beneath the porch with lattice. The techniques for installing a lattice skirt also apply to using lattice on a deck, fence, gate, privacy screen, or trellis.

The skirt is actually a series of frames with lattice applied to them. The completed frames of a lattice porch skirt should be ½ inch narrower than the width of each opening (measured from column to column or post to post) and 1 inch shorter than the height of each opening.

The porch shown here has five 26-inch-high openings between posts, ranging from 8½ to 9½ feet across. Because manufactured lattice panels are only 8 feet long, vertical braces are used to conceal the seams between adjoining panels. If your porch's openings are 8 feet or less, these vertical braces are unnecessary.

The frames and braces are made from pressure-treated lumber, although all-heart redwood or cedar may also be used. When buying the lumber, choose the straightest and driest boards with the fewest knots. The frames are 1 by 6s ripped to 4½ inches; the braces are 1 by 4s.

The lattice used for the project shown is high-density polyethylene, which resists decay, splitting, and mildew; it comes in six colors and three basic patterns. Wood lattice, which can be painted to match siding or trim colors, is also widely available.

TIP: Leave one panel unobstructed for easy access to storage beneath the porch.

1 Remove the old porch skirt with a flat pry bar. If necessary, cut the skirt in pieces with a reciprocating saw.

2 Assemble the frame for each opening. Hold together each corner joint with a 6-inch mending plate and a 3½-inch flat corner brace attached with ¾-inch outdoor screws.

3 Attach a center brace to each frame using two T-plates. Fasten the plates to the frame with ¾-inch outdoor screws.

4 Connect the lattice to each frame with 1-inch panhead outdoor screws and washers. Drill slightly oversized screw holes through the lattice to allow for expansion and contraction.

5 Secure the edges wherever two adjoining lattice panels meet over a center brace with a double row of panhead outdoor screws and washers.

6 Fasten each lattice frame to the porch's horizontal trim or fascia with 3-inch galvanized T-hinges. Level the soil to ensure that each panel will swing up and down freely and allow easy access below the porch.

Windows

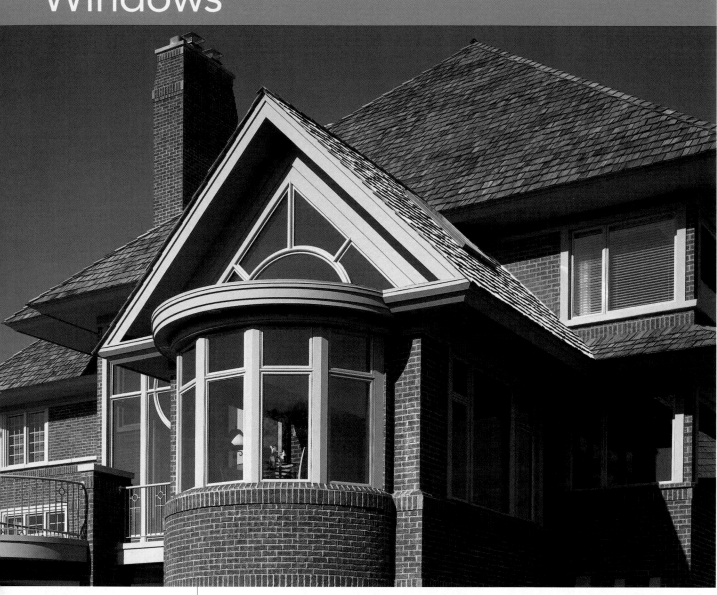

A bow-shaped series of windows capped by a triangular specialty window make a dramatic architectural statement.

Windows are part of a home's architectural identity, immediately conveying its period, style, and quality. Windows that don't suit a home's architecture, that look dated or cheaply made, or that cry out for a coat of paint can seriously detract from a house's appearance, both outside and inside.

If the only thing your windows need is a little paint, see page 130. If window boxes may add just the right splash of color and style, see the project on page 124. If you need to replace your existing windows with new ones, the following information will help you sort through the options to make the best choices.

When choosing new windows, be sure the styles you select will suit your home both aesthetically and practically. How they look is only half the issue; windows have a tremendous environmental influence on a house, affecting the light, ventilation, and temperature inside.

Windows come in hundreds of shapes, sizes, and types and are made from a variety of materials. When selecting windows, consider your home's style, each window's performance, and, of course, your budget. Weigh the importance of ventilation and security, and think about each style's ease of maintenance. Also consider whether you want the windows to be fixed or operable.

New windows are a major investment, so it is important to shop around. Search manufacturers' Web sites. Visit home improvement centers, local distributors of major window manufacturers, and millwork shops. Nearly every major manufacturer offers a catalog that shows the entire line of windows—ask for these catalogs and study them. From this information, you can gain a clear understanding of the differences between various window types—casement versus double-hung, for example—materials, sizes, prices, and more.

Manufacturers' catalogs, however, may not help you sort through the benefits and drawbacks of particular materials. The following information will help you gain a clearer idea of the features to consider.

Materials

Windows are made from wood, aluminum, steel, vinyl, or fiberglass—or from combinations of these materials. In general, windows that offer better weather protection cost more, but they pay off in low maintenance and energy savings.

Wood Wood is the most popular material for the parts of a window that are seen from indoors. It does not conduct cold or allow for condensation as much as other materials do. Wood, however, is subject to shrinkage and swelling, which means it can warp and rot over time—especially on the exterior—if it is not well protected.

Unless you order wood windows finished or primed, they typically come unfinished. If you intend to paint them, you can purchase them already primed on the exterior and interior surfaces of the frame and sash. Certain manufacturers offer pre-painted wood windows, though color choices are limited.

Some windows that appear to be wood on the inside are actually composites that have been given a surface veneer of wood or a layer of embossed cellulose that looks like wood. These will take a stain beautifully and perform better than all-wood windows.

Clad wood Many new windows are made mostly of wood but are clad on the outside with tough aluminum or vinyl. The cladding, which covers both sash and frame, will keep windows virtually maintenance-free for years. Cladding is typically available in a few stock colors. With vinyl, the color permeates the material, so scratches don't show. Aluminum is tougher, but it will scratch; it is available in a wider variety of colors and is easier to paint (though neither vinyl nor aluminum should require painting). Neither type will rust or rot.

Vinyl-clad casement windows with full divided light grills are available in many custom shapes.

These aluminum-clad windows are as strong as they are beautiful—high-tech laminated glass helps them stand up to hurricane-force winds.

Aluminum Aluminum windows look at home with certain types of architecture—most notably contemporary. Aluminum windows are more durable, lighter in weight, and easier to handle during installation than wood windows. To reduce heat loss and condensation, quality models are insulated with a thermal break of extruded vinyl and, sometimes, foam. Finishes protect the aluminum from corrosion but deteriorate in the salty air of coastal areas.

Vinyl Vinyl windows are made from rigid, impact-resistant polyvinyl chloride (PVC) and have hollow spaces inside to make them resistant to heat loss and condensation. Inexpensive vinyl windows have a tendency to distort when exposed to extreme heat or cold, making them harder to operate and allowing for air leakage. Vinyl windows cannot be painted, and darker shades may fade over time.

Steel Steel is more resistant to the elements than both aluminum and wood, but steel windows generally are not used in homes because of their expense. If you have the budget, they are attractive, low-maintenance, and durable.

Window Construction

Most wood windows come pre-hung in complete frames. They are attached with nails driven through the exterior casing, or brickmold, and through the jambs. Vinyl or aluminum windows and some wood windows with a vinyl or aluminum cladding have a factory-installed nailing flange on the outside that you can attach to the perimeter of the window's rough framing.

Window Hardware

All operable windows come equipped with hardware—the mechanisms used for opening and closing the sash, the latches, and so forth.

Casement, awning, and hopper styles are opened and closed with a crank. Some manufacturers offer cranks in nonmetallic finishes (notably white), and some new types have an inconspicuous fold-down handle.

Latches on the frame are used to hold the window tightly closed. Tall or wide hinged windows use two latches. Keyed sash locks can make a window more secure.

Window Glazing

The surest and most effective way to prevent wasting energy in a home is to utilize high-performance glazing in windows and doors.

Window Styles

For a remodel, it's safest to choose window styles in keeping with the predominant type used in the rest of the house. Double-hung windows, which slide open from both the top and the bottom, are appropriate for almost any type of house, particularly period styles such as Craftsman and Colonial. Casement windows, which swing outward to open, have a more contemporary look, although the addition of muntins can make them seem more traditional. Awning windows also have a more modern appearance; because they open from the top of the window frame, they're often placed high on a wall for ventilation. Sliding windows work best with ranch houses and other architectural styles that have strong horizontal lines. Picture windows, which can't be opened, can create a large expanse of glass that looks quite contemporary, but smaller sizes with muntins and specialty shapes can complement traditional styles.

Two important ratings to check when buying windows and glazed doors are the R-value and the U-value. An R-value measures a material's resistance to heat transfer; the higher the R-value, the better the insulating properties of the glazing. The U-value measures overall energy efficiency. It tells you the rate at which heat flows through the entire window or door, frame and all. The lower the U-value, the more energy-efficient the window or door. An average U-value is fine for warm climates; in cold climates, a lower U-value is worth the premium you are likely to pay for it.

Insulating glazing typically has two, or sometimes three, panes of glass sealed together, with either air or argon gas trapped between them as an insulator. Some units have a plastic film suspended between two glass panes. If the unit is properly sealed, condensation should not occur between the panes. One important reason for buying windows and doors with a strong warranty is to ensure they will be backed if the seal fails and condensation occurs (there is no easy way to get rid of condensation in dual glazing).

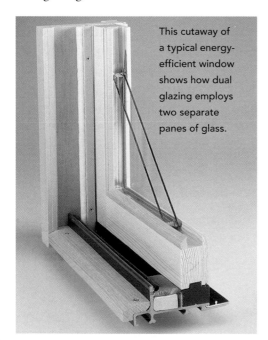

This cutaway of a typical energy-efficient window shows how dual glazing employs two separate panes of glass.

Replacement Windows

The traditional look of wooden double-hung windows has an enduring appeal. However, old double-hung windows are infamous for becoming drafty, inefficient, and unattractive as their sashes deteriorate with age. Few things can detract from a house's appearance like poorly maintained windows.

Completely replacing windows can be expensive because the trim and jambs must be removed, the rough opening often needs to be restructured, and, in many cases, both the siding and the interior wall covering must be repaired. Instead of going through this expense and hassle, however, you can revamp a window by replacing only the sash with a special replacement window made to fit into the existing frame.

Replacement windows are made by major window manufacturers and are available through window retailers and home improvement centers. You can have them professionally installed, or you can buy sash replacement kits that can be easily installed by experienced do-it-yourselfers.

In addition to standard-size models, replacement windows can be custom ordered to fit most frames. Kits come with all of the installation hardware required and complete instructions. Most types require only a handful of commonly available tools, such as a hammer, screwdriver, and power drill.

With most kits, you remove the old sash after prying out the stop. Then you take off the old jamb hardware, and replace it with new metal channels that fit the replacement sash. You put the new sash into the opening (as shown above), and finally, nail the stops in place along the side jambs.

Project: Building a Window Box

This easy-to-build box perks up a window with style and seasonal color.

When it comes to adding charm to a home's facade, few design elements can rival a window box. Window boxes can be made from a range of materials to complement most any home style or siding type. Their versatility comes from the vast array of flowers, herbs, ferns, and vegetables they can house.

As eye-catching as window boxes can be, they can also quickly become eyesores if plantings are not well tended. For this reason, they work best on double-hung windows or on casement windows that open in, both of which provide easy access to these mini-gardens. In addition, affixing window boxes (see Hanging a Window Box, opposite) by attaching wire to the window casings will allow for easy removal.

For best appearance, a window box should be the same length as the window's width, including trim. It should be 7 to 8 inches wide and deep enough to adequately accommodate plant roots. The obvious advantage of making your own is that you can choose the materials and decorate it any way you wish to accent your house and trim.

The box shown here is 32 inches long and about 8 inches deep. It's made from a 10-foot-long clear white pine 1 by 10—a costly grade that is worth the price because there are no knots to bleed through a paint finish. If you are choosing plantings that will largely cover the box, you can choose a less expensive grade of wood. For better resistance to decay, the box can also be made of cedar or redwood.

The ends of this box are tapered at a 10-degree angle to provide a touch of visual interest. Three pairs of holes ½ inch in diameter are equally spaced along the bottom to allow for drainage.

1 Cut out all the pieces, and mark the ends so they taper from 7 inches at the bottom to 8⁷⁄₁₆ inches at the top. Cut along these lines.

2 Glue and screw the pieces together, using exterior-grade glue and 1½-inch trim-head screws. Set the screws slightly below the wood's surface.

3 Fill the screw countersinks with an exterior putty such as a two-part polyester filler. After the filler has cured, sand it flush.

4 Apply a clear wood preservative to the inside and a top-quality primer and two coats of 100 percent acrylic paint to the outside.

Hanging a Window Box

If your house has a windowsill deep enough for a flower box to sit on the top of it, just set the box on spacers so water can drain freely from the bottom. If, as is more common, your window-sills are not that deep, you can attach a window box in several ways. The trick is to make sure the window box does not trap water against the house siding.

On wood- or vinyl-sided houses, install a pair of sturdy metal brackets to the siding using galvanized or stainless-steel screws, and leave a ⅟₁₆-inch clear-ance between the box and the siding. For masonry walls, wedge or sleeve anchors should do the job.

Another method is to set the back edge of the window box on the sill and secure it with a steel cable attached to the window casing.

Last, attach the box to the front edge of the sill with T-shaped galvanized brackets. Screw the long leg to the back of the box and the short leg to the sill.

TIP: To prevent the wood from splitting, first drill pilot holes for the screws.

Paint

A deep-blue door, turquoise trim, and magenta walls establish the tone and character of this dazzling Southwest-style home.

One of the quickest, easiest, and least expensive ways to give a house a new lease on life is to paint it. New paint will renew and protect weathered siding and trim and can add significantly to a house's style and distinction.

The most common types of paint for exterior surfaces are water-base (latex) and oil-base (alkyd). Primers, wood stains, and clear finishes also are available in both latex and alkyd formulations. The chief advantage of high-quality, relatively expensive products is that they offer better "hiding," meaning fewer coats, and better washability.

Whether you choose alkyd or latex, flat paint is best on siding for resisting moisture, while semigloss or gloss paint is best for trim and doors because of its durability and contrast.

Siding stains are available in transparent, semitransparent, and solid-hide latex and alkyd formulations. Transparent formulations are typically used only on cedar and redwood, which are naturally rot-resistant woods.

Latex

Latex paint accounts for the vast majority of house paints sold today, and for good reason: It cleans up with soap and water, dries quickly, resists yellowing with age, and poses the least threat to the environment. In addition, latex paint dries to a porous finish, allowing moisture in wood to evaporate through the paint film, which prevents peeling.

The type of resin used in the formula determines the quality of latex paint. The highest-quality and most durable latex paints contain 100 percent acrylic resin. Vinyl acrylic and other blends are next in quality. Paint containing solely vinyl resin is the least durable and lowest quality of the available latex formulations—avoid it.

While all-acrylic paints are more expensive than those containing vinyl, they offer better adhesion, gloss, and color retention.

Latex paint usually is dry to the touch in 30 minutes and in warm, dry weather, is resistant to light showers or dew after about four hours.

Alkyd

Alkyd paints, or solvent-base paints, level out better than latexes, drying virtually free of brush marks for a smooth, hard finish. They are a wise choice for painting over glossy surfaces because they offer better adhesion. Alkyd paints, however, are harder to apply, tend to sag more, and take longer to dry than latex paints. They also require cleanup with paint thinner.

Alkyd house paint contains solvents that evaporate into the air as volatile organic compounds (VOCs), causing pollution. For this reason, it is not available in states that have stringent air-quality regulations. In some cases, it is available only in quart cans, making it expensive to use as a coating for exterior siding. As a result, alkyd paints are generally reserved for trim or used as a primer on bare or poorly prepared wood, where adhesion can be a problem.

You need a primer when the surface to be painted is porous or when applying latex over existing alkyd paint or alkyd over existing latex paint. An alkyd primer can be applied over either alkyd or latex paint.

Alkyd paints usually are dry to the touch in four to six hours and are dry enough to recoat in eight to 12 hours. They will continue to harden for several months after application.

TIP: If you want a new paint job to last for years, never cut corners on preparation or paint quality.

Finishes for Exterior Surfaces

This chart does not recommend the use of primers in most cases—for a number of reasons. Wood doesn't need primer if it will be stained. Vinyl or aluminum siding is sufficiently covered with two coats of acrylic latex. With brick, stucco, and concrete, the first latex finish coat performs the function of a primer.

SURFACE	PRIMER	FINISH
Wood or plywood siding	Alkyd	2 coats alkyd paint, flat/semigloss/gloss
	Latex	2 coats latex paint, flat/semigloss/gloss
	None	2 coats latex stain, solid hide
	None	2 coats alkyd stain, solid hide/semitransparent
Hardboard siding	Alkyd	2 coats latex paint, semigloss/gloss
Wood trim	Latex	2 coats latex paint, semigloss/gloss
	Alkyd	2 coats alkyd paint, flat/semigloss/gloss
Vinyl or aluminum siding	None	2 coats acrylic latex paint, flat/semigloss/gloss
Brick	None	2 coats latex paint, flat
Block	Latex block filler	2 coats latex paint, flat
Stucco	None	2 coats latex paint, flat
Concrete	None	2 coats latex paint, flat

TIP: Puncture the paint can's rim in two or three places so the paint won't pool and spill over the edge.

Painting Safety

Although paint is relatively user-friendly, exercise caution when working with it. Following are some basic guidelines for painting safely:

■ Wear a dust mask and safety goggles when sanding to keep from breathing in dust particles and to protect your eyes.

■ Wear safety goggles when using chemical strippers or caustic cleaning compounds or when painting overhead.

■ Be especially careful when handling or applying products that contain solvents. Wear safety goggles, gloves, and a respirator when called for by label directions.

■ Inspect ladders for sturdiness. Make sure the legs rest squarely on the ground and the cross braces are locked in place. Never stand on the top step or the utility shelf. Never lean away from a ladder; get off and move it if you can't reach a spot easily.

■ For scaffolding planks, use 2 by 10s no more than 12 feet long. If you place the planks between two ladders, position the ladders so their steps are facing each other. If you run planks between ladders or between a ladder and a sawhorse, make sure the planks are level and secure.

■ Clean up promptly after painting, and properly dispose of soiled rags. To eliminate any chance of spontaneous combustion, spread rags soaked with alkyd paint or thinner outdoors and let them dry all day before disposing of them at a toxic-waste dump. Don't leave rags to dry in areas accessible to children or pets.

Paint Failure

Before repainting a house, it's important to determine whether the existing paint has deteriorated because of problems beyond basic wear and weathering. Unless you fix systemic problems, the same troubles may resurface with your new paint job. Here is a close look at typical symptoms and how to handle them.

Mildew Mildew is a fungus that grows on cool, damp surfaces, showing up as black spots. To treat mildew, wash the area with a solution of ⅔ cup TSP (trisodium phosphate), ⅓ cup detergent, 1 quart household bleach, and 3 quarts warm water. Be sure to wear rubber gloves and eye protection when preparing and applying the solution.

Chalking Chalking is the normal breakdown of a paint finish after long exposure to sunlight. To treat chalking, wash off the loose, powdery material and repaint.

Wrinkling Wrinkling is caused by applying a coat of paint over another that isn't thoroughly dry or by applying a coat too heavily. To treat wrinkling, allow the paint to dry thoroughly, sand off the wrinkles, and repaint.

Blistering Blistering can be caused by moisture invading the subsurface of paint through cracked boards or poor caulking or by the lack of a vapor barrier. Blistering also can be caused by the use of oil-base paints in hot weather, which can trap solvents. In either case, scrape and sand the blistered paint, repair any sources of moisture, and then repaint in cool weather.

Peeling on windowsills Properly designed sills slope away from the window to prevent water from pooling. Still, heavy rains or sprinklers can allow moisture to permeate the wood, causing peeling and cracks. To treat peeling, sand the sills down to the bare wood, prime them with alkyd primer, fill all cracks with paintable caulk, and apply two coats of finish paint.

Inter-coat peeling Applying latex finish coats over surfaces previously painted with gloss alkyd often results in poor adhesion. Sand off the latex paint, prime the surface with an alkyd primer, and then apply latex finish coats. Some top-of-the-line acrylic paints can

The ornate trim of this vintage Victorian sets a playful, whimsical tone thanks to meticulous multicolored painting.

be applied over old alkyd paint without the need for priming, but thorough sanding is required to give the surface "bite."

Multiple-coat peeling Structures that have been painted over many times, especially with oil-base paints, sometimes will show paint failure down to the bare wood. This is caused by the paint layers becoming brittle and then cracking as the wood below expands and contracts with temperature changes. These cracks allow moisture to enter and cause peeling. Strip the surface down to the bare wood, and prepare as you would new wood before repainting.

Grain cracking on plywood When plywood is repeatedly exposed to moisture, the surface develops cracks as the wood expands and contracts. Once cracked, repair is not possible. Treat this problem by replacing the plywood, priming it with an exterior-grade primer, and then painting with at least two coats of alkyd or latex finish.

Project: Painting Trim

Carefully painted and well-maintained window trim is a true hallmark of quality.

When it comes to damage from sun, rain, and wind, one of a house's most susceptible elements is its wood trim. Fortunately, a new coat of paint can turn around this deterioration and make a house look great again.

The key to a top-notch paint job is preparation. In fact, if you hire a painter to resurrect your trim, 80 percent of the time—and your expense—will be spent preparing the surfaces properly. At the very least, preparation involves a thorough cleaning, light sanding, and priming. It may also require scraping, stripping, reglazing, wire brushing, filling, and caulking. *Warning:* If you use a heat gun to remove old paint (below), be sure to first read the manufacturer's safety instructions.

Start by scrubbing off all dirt and chalking paint with a scrub brush and a solution of trisodium phosphate (TSP). Rinse the trim thoroughly, and allow it to dry completely before

1 Remove any badly damaged trim, and replace it.

2 Disc sand the fascia, graduating from rough- to fine-grit paper.

3 Blister the paint with a heat gun, and peel it away with a putty knife. *See safety note above.*

preparing the surfaces for primer and final coats of paint.

Primer seals the surface and provides a base to which the paint can adhere well. Slow-drying alkyd-base primers are your best bet. On partially bare wood, apply two coats of primer. To help the paint cover, have your paint dealer tint the primer with some of the finish color.

Considering the relatively low-cost, yet critical function of paint in protecting your house, it does not make sense to skimp on paint quality. When you buy good paint, not only will your paint job last longer, but the paint will also go on more smoothly. If you have prepared the surfaces carefully, as detailed here, an acrylic latex paint is your best choice for a topcoat. A good latex paint will actually hold its color and sheen longer than an alkyd-base paint, and because it is water-base, cleanup is infinitely easier.

Last but not least, paint when the weather is moderately warm and winds are calm. Painting in heat or under direct sun will cause the paint to dry too quickly, weakening its bond. Rain can ruin paint that has not dried.

4 Tap out old window glazing compound that is cracked or brittle.

5 Power sand the windowsills, graduating from rough- to fine-grit paper.

TIP: If you suspect that old paint may contain lead, have it tested before sanding or stripping it.

6 Fill cracks and holes with a vinyl spackling compound, and sand the surface when it is dry.

7 Spread new glazing compound on the trim at an angle, and let it cure.

8 Paint the window trim, holding a sash brush to apply the paint as shown.

An antique iron gate, stone pillars, and rustic wooden pickets join to give this home a warm, well-aged appearance.

When it comes to curb appeal, the old adage "Good fences make good neighbors" rings true. Fences serve a variety of purposes: They provide privacy, improve security, keep kids and dogs in the yard, and define a property's area. But they can also make a front yard more beautiful and, as a result, perk up the neighborhood. The right fence and gate can underscore a home's architecture, add character and style to the yard, and call out a view of the front yard worth emphasizing. For more about fences and gates, see page 62.

Most fences and gates are made either entirely of wood or of wood used in concert with other materials. The versatility of wood as a fencing material is reflected in the wide variety of

Left: White painted pickets united by a solid horizontal top rail and accented with ball-shaped post caps make this refined fence the perfect backdrop for seasonal color.

Below: Low horizontal board fencing produces a country-ranch feel.
Bottom: Rough-hewn pickets make a back-to-nature fence.

its forms, which include rough-hewn split rails and grape stakes, smooth dimension lumber, round poles, and more.

All wood used for fence building should be decay-resistant. In particular, wood that comes in contact with the ground is susceptible to decay from moisture and termite attack, so it should be pressure-treated with a wood preservative or cut from the heartwood of a decay-resistant species such as cedar or redwood. Wood used for above-ground parts of fences should be protected from weather by paint, stain, or wood preservative.

Pre-cut fence boards and pickets are commonly available at lumberyards and home improvement centers. You can buy pre-assembled fence sections, too, with rails already attached. These usually come pre-primed. When buying wood, pay attention to the grade and quality of the material. Avoid pieces that are warped, twisted, cupped, split, or perforated with loose or open knots.

Metal is also a popular fence and gate material because of its strength and durability. A talented metal worker can form and weld steel rods, pipes, bars, heavy wire, or prefabricated fence sections into remarkably beautiful designs. Of course, metal will rust if untreated, so, unless the rusted look is what you are after, be sure to coat metal with a metal primer and apply a durable topcoat

Top: A sawtooth pattern of short and tall pickets embues this fence with a distinctive style.
Above: A custom-made wood door and bold arbor provide an elegant, private entry.
Right: Wood lattice fencing gives visual relief to the top of this stucco wall.

of rust-resistant paint. Depending upon the fence's design, a spray-on paint may be the easiest to apply.

Plywood panels, wood shingles, and wood lattice sections are just a few other materials that make good fences. Even chain-link fencing can be attractive when it is used as a trellis for a dense wall of vines. Vinyl or composite fencing, which will not rust, is sold in 4-by-4 and 4-by-8 panels that look like lattice, pickets, or certain types of board fencing. Colors, which will not peel or require repainting because they are integral to the material rather than applied as a coating, are limited to basic white and light to medium shades of brown, gray, and green.

Gates are often crafted from the same materials used in the fence, and most home improvement centers sell gate kits that match their prefabricated fence offerings. But remember that because a gate is often the first thing visitors encounter, it may be worth the premium to have a distinctive gate designed and built by a skilled woodworker or craftsperson.

Top: This light and airy fence and gate employ a combination of wood, steel, and wire.
Above: A handcrafted gate is the ideal complement to rustic reed fencing.

Project: Building a Fence

The tops of this classic fence's pickets were cut to produce curves that sweep from post to post.

1 Measure the fence run, and drive a stake to mark each end post. Then run mason's twine between the stakes, draw it tight, and tie it firmly.

2 Locate the intermediate posts, and use a plumb bob to establish the center of each post's position. Mark the spot with a nail and a piece of paper.

Though wood fences can vary widely in form and function, nearly all are constructed from the same basic parts—a framework of vertical posts and horizontal rails that is sided with pickets or boards.

Building most fences is a three-stage process. First is the relatively easy task of plotting the fence. Next comes the more arduous step of installing the posts. And last is the straightforward stage of attaching the rails and siding.

Before you build a fence, it's a good idea to check out local building and zoning codes, which may dictate heights, setbacks, and other specifications. This is a must if the fence is planned along property lines. In that case, it's advisable to have a surveyor or civil engineer lay out the corner stakes. And check on the locations of underground pipes and cables with your utility company before digging holes for posts.

For a long-lasting fence, use pressure-treated wood or high-quality, all-heart redwood, cedar, or cypress. Make sure all the connectors you use—such as screws, nails, bolts, and brackets—are galvanized.

The typical wooden fence, whether sided with solid boards or open pickets, generally has 4-by-4 posts placed on 6-foot centers and 2-by-4 rails between the posts. Whether for a 3-foot-tall picket fence or a 5-foot-tall board fence, posts typically are sunk into concrete at least 2 feet below ground.

Most home centers and lumber dealers carry ready-made fence boards, pickets, and post caps. For something with a bit more character, you can cut your own.

Setting Fence Posts in Concrete

1 With a posthole digger or auger, dig holes 6 inches deeper than the posts will go and 2½ to 3 times the diameter of each post. Add 4 to 6 inches of gravel to each hole, center a post in each hole, and shovel in pre-mixed posthole concrete. Fill the hole until the concrete is an inch above ground.

2 To hold each post while the concrete sets, make braces from 1 by 4s and short stakes. Fasten the braces to two adjacent sides of the post.

3 Use a water level or mason's twine and a line level to mark the heights of the posts. Once the concrete is set, use a reciprocating saw to cut each post to the proper height.

Attaching the Rails and Boards or Pickets

1 Use a square to make sure each rail is perpendicular to the posts, and then fasten the rail to the posts by toenailing or using angle or fence-rail brackets.

2 Cut the boards or pickets to length, and then stretch a level line from post to post to mark the bottom of the boards or pickets. Check each board or picket for plumb, and then secure it to the rails with galvanized screws or nails that are roughly three times as long as the board's thickness.

3 To ensure the uniform spacing and height of successive pickets on a picket fence, make a spacer slat. Cut the slat to the exact length of the pickets. Attach a small cleat to the back of the slat. The slat, when hung on the top rail, should be even with the pickets.

TIP: You can cut simple pointed pickets with a handsaw, but for more intricate designs, use a power saber saw, or jig saw. Make a master pattern first, and then trace it on the boards to be cut.

Relatively easy to build, this attractive gate offers security yet extends a welcome to visitors.

A gate is essentially a frame with siding that mounts to a post with hinges. A perimeter frame, like the one shown here, is strong enough for pickets and will even hold heavier board siding. For gates with standard 2-by-4 framing and 4-by-4 posts, plan to leave ½ inch between the latch post and the gate frame so the gate can swing without rubbing. The clearance space needed on the hinge side will depend on the type of hinges you use; ¼ inch is sufficient for most gate hinges.

The main consideration when hanging a gate is making sure the hinges and their fasteners are strong enough to hold the gate's weight. Screws should penetrate the gate frame and the gatepost as far as possible without coming out the other side.

Latches come in a number of types and styles. Regardless of the type you choose, make sure the parts align with both the gate frame and the latch post. Again, use screws that penetrate as far as possible without coming out the other side.

To ensure the gate does not swing too far when it closes (which can loosen the hinges), fasten a strip of wood vertically to either the gate frame or the latch post.

Building a Gate

1 Cut the frame pieces to length. For strength, use rabbet joints (notches across the ends of boards). Cut the rabbets at both ends of the horizontal frame pieces. Assemble the frame pieces on a flat work surface. For maximum strength, fasten the pieces with deck screws and weatherproof glue instead of nails. Use a carpenter's square to make sure the boards are perpendicular to each other as you join them.

2 Set the gate frame on top of a 2 by 4 positioned diagonally from the bottom hinge-side corner to the top latch-side corner. Mark the inside corners on the 2 by 4 as shown, and cut along the outside of the pencil marks.

3 Test fit the brace and check that the frame corners are still at 90 degrees. Trim the brace ends, if necessary. Drill pilot holes through the frame into the brace ends, and then drive fasteners through the frame pieces into the ends of the brace.

4 Lay out the boards or pickets and test their fit to the frame. Then nail on the pieces or attach them with screws, starting at the hinge side. It's simplest to let the board tops run long and then cut them all at once.

Hanging a Gate

1 Position the hinges on the gate frame, mark the screw holes, and drill a pilot hole at each mark. Then screw the hinges to the frame.

2 Prop the gate in position using wood blocks and shims, and then mark the screw holes on the gate-post. Drill pilot holes for the screws, and then fasten the hinges to the gatepost. Remove the shims and blocks, test the swing, and adjust the gate if needed.

3 Hold the latch in place on the latch post, drill pilot holes, and screw in the latch. Insert the strike into the latch, and similarly attach it to the gate frame.

Lawns & Ground Covers

BEFORE & AFTER An artful mix of lawn, grasses, and ground cover softens the formal facade of this house.

A t one time, the ideal of suburban perfection was a house surrounded by a large plot of immaculately maintained lawn. The lawn is still a powerful and compelling image, one that suits many formal architectural styles. Today, however, many home owners are opting to limit, or eliminate entirely, the front lawn.

The reasons are many. Lawns are insatiable consumers of water and fertilizer and demand a lot of care. Design trends have changed, as well—more people are using water-conserving native plants and desiring variety and a natural, casual look in the front yard. And with space at a premium, many home owners are recapturing front-yard space for courtyards, outdoor entertaining areas, carports, and parking.

Still, the lawn can have a very valuable place in front-yard landscaping. With its uniform height and color, a deep green lawn is the perfect foil for exuberant flower beds, trees, and shrubs. The lawn separates and demarcates beds and pathways and brings balance to the overall landscape scheme. On a practical level, it provides a cushioned surface for front-yard play

and an outdoor carpet for lounging. A properly handled lawn can be a versatile, and even indispensable, design element.

The historic popularity of lawns has led to the great profusion of grasses available today, sold either as seed, sod, sprigs, or plugs. Grasses, which come as single-type cultivars, blends of several cultivars of the same species, or mixes of different species, vary greatly in appearance and in maintenance, water, sun, and climate zone needs. There are warm- and cool-season grasses, grasses that prefer sun or shade, delicate grasses, and hardy grasses fit for a football field. There are even native grasses, eye-catching for their lack of uniform growth, which look wonderful with rustic homes but have short growing seasons. The grass you choose for your lawn will depend on several factors: how you will use the lawn, the amount of shade the lawn will receive, and where you live. Once you sort out the first two issues, your local nursery or county agricultural office can advise you of grass options appropriate for your area and your needs.

Grass grows best on a flat surface. If your front yard is hilly or sloped, you may want to consider other landscape options, such as ground cover.

A healthy lawn depends on solid preparation. You should grade the lawn area, provide it with good drainage, and, for convenience, possibly install an automatic sprinkler system. The soil itself deserves attention. You will want to have the soil analyzed and the plot thoroughly amended before planting.

Once the lawn is established, it will require regular maintenance. Most lawns need mowing, and the mower blade height requirement and frequency will vary by type of grass as well as by season. If the soil is well prepared, you will probably not need to fertilize very often, if at all, although there are plenty of fertilizer options available at local home and garden centers. The lawn should

receive regular watering, either naturally or through an irrigation system. Water deeply to encourage deep root growth, which will serve a lawn well during hot summer months. Be alert to signs of disease or pests, and deal with them swiftly because small problems can compound and wipe out your lawn in no time. Dethatching, removing the layer of brownish-yellow fibrous material that builds up on the soil surface, and aerating, punching holes through the lawn and into the ground below to facilitate the flow

Creeping fescue grows well on banks or mounds, and creates a lush effect when left unmowed.

For steep slopes, ground cover prevents erosion while adding splashes of color to the landscape.

An expanse of lawn gains interest when broken up by "islands" of shrubbery.

Some Common Grasses

WARM SEASON:

Common or hybrid Bermuda: Tolerates sun; is drought-, pest-, and disease-resistant; has low tolerance for cold and shade. Wearability: good.

Bahia grass: Takes sun or part shade; tolerates sandy or less than perfect soil. Wearability: very good.

Zoysia grass: Tolerates some shade, heat, drought, disease, and pests. Wearability: good.

COOL SEASON:

Kentucky bluegrass: Tolerates cold and some shade but does need a good deal of water; is resistant to disease. Wearability: moderate.

Annual ryegrass: Often used to overseed warm-season grass lawns in mild-winter areas; tolerates cold, shade, and wet conditions. Wearability: moderate.

Fescues (Chewings, Creeping Red, Sheep's, Hard): Adapts to all soil conditions except for clay soil; tolerates dry conditions. Wearability: poor to moderate.

of water and oxygen, are important annual or biannual maintenance jobs to keep the lawn fresh and healthy.

When designing the lawn, you will have many options. Lawns can fill the entire front yard or be carved into any number of shapes to create striking effects. The deep green can seem like a sea that laps against flower- and tree-filled islands. Maintain a good proportion of lawn to beds to prevent either from looking skimpy.

If you opt to combine the lawn, trees, flower beds, and walkway, there are a few rules of thumb. Make sure to keep the lawn at least 3 feet wide at all points to facilitate mowing. Installing mowing strips or edgings to the beds also makes the job easier and helps to keep grass growth in check, particularly for varieties that spread by runners. Because most grass needs some sun, leave any area of deep shade, such as the space under a mature tree, as a bed for shade plants, rocks, or wood chips. You can use the lawn to direct foot traffic around flower

beds, but keep in mind that the more foot traffic you encourage, the hardier the species of grass you will need to install.

If a hilly lot precludes a lawn, or if you simply would rather go without a lawn, a mix of ground cover and flower beds may be just the ticket. A well-planted ground cover can provide the same visual uniformity as a lawn and generally needs less continuous care. Ground covers, small plants that propagate and spread to cover a surface, come in a range of heights, foliage and flower colors, and textures and have a variety of water, sun, and feeding requirements. Some low-growing ground covers also can tolerate a bit of foot traffic and work well between paving stones. Again, a local nursery will be able to advise you on the best choices for your particular conditions. As with lawns, make sure the plot has proper drainage, grading, and soil amendment. Be on the lookout for pests, diseases, and invasive weeds, which can quickly take over a bed and turn it into an eyesore rather than an asset.

Above: A shapeless front yard becomes a low-maintenance beauty with a softly curving lawn ringed by liriope ground cover.

This front-yard design incorporates a sculpted St. Augustine lawn to serve as an overflow area for entertaining.

A lustrous carpet of lawn requires the right choice of grass and a simple regimen of feeding, watering, and mowing.

I f it's time to give your home a new lawn, your first decision will be whether to sow seed, lay sod, or plant sprigs or plugs. The method you choose will depend upon your climate, budget, patience, and the type of grass you want, as discussed on pages 140–143.

The key to establishing a successful lawn is preparation. The area should first be raked so that it slopes gently away from the house and any other structures that could be damaged by standing water. A 3-inch slope for every 10 feet, or about 2½ feet for every 100 feet, is generally sufficient. In addition, the area should be graded so that it appears even overall.

Next, the soil should be tested to determine its acidity or alkalinity. If the soil is highly acidic, add ground limestone. If the soil is highly alkaline, add iron sulfate or elemental sulfur. If you need to bring in additional soil, make sure it matches the adjusted pH of your amended soil.

After adjusting the pH of your soil, add organic nitrogen-stabilizing soil amendments. Make sure all amendments and any additional soil are mixed together thoroughly with the existing soil. If you cultivate the area too finely, however, the surface can form a crust, making it difficult for seedlings or roots to penetrate.

Most lawns grown from seed are cool-weather lawns, while sprigs or plugs are most often used for warm-weather lawns. Sod comes in both cool- and warm-weather varieties, but the range of grasses is not as wide as with seed or sprigs.

Spring is the optimum time to put in a new lawn of any type. After installation, water daily (more frequently if the weather turns very hot) for at least six weeks. Cut the grass for the first time when it has grown a third taller than its ideal height.

Sowing From Seed

Rake and level the area. Firm the soil with a roller, first in one direction and then perpendicular to the initial stroke. Do a final leveling with a garden rake.

1 Work organic amendments deep into the soil with a rotary tiller.

2 Scatter the seed and lawn fertilizer evenly.

3 Lightly rake the seed into the soil.

4 Spread ¼ inch of mulch, and then press the seed into the soil using an empty roller.

TIP: If weeds emerge, don't attempt to control them until you have mowed the young lawn four times. By this stage, many weeds will have been killed by mowing or crowded out by the new growing lawn.

Planting Sprigs or Plugs

A sprig (below) is a grass stem with roots and blades, usually sold by the bushel. Scatter sprigs evenly over the soil, and then roll them with a cleated roller.

A plug (above) is a small square or circle of sod usually sold 18 to a tray. Ask your supplier how much area each amount will cover. Plant plugs 8 to 12 inches apart, on center, in soil that has been well prepared.

Laying Sod

Schedule the delivery of sod so you will have enough time to plant the entire area in a single day. Early morning is usually best to avoid the mid-day heat.

1 Unroll the strips over well-moistened, prepared soil, laying them in brick-bond fashion, and press the edges together firmly.

2 Trim the sod using a sharp knife to fit it snugly around paving and odd-shaped areas.

3 Roll the lawn with a roller half filled with water to smooth out rough spots and press the roots firmly into the soil.

Planting Ground Cover

As with a new lawn, new ground cover requires careful preparation of the planting area. Remove weeds, amend the soil with
compost or manure, and broadcast a complete fertilizer over
the area. Work the amendments and fertilizer in with a shovel,
or a tiller if the area is vast, and then rake to level the soil.

Space the ground cover according to the recommendations
for the particular plant and according to how quickly you want
the growth to cover the area. Set each plant in a hole just deep
enough for and slightly wider than the root ball.

Set the ground-cover plants in a diamond pattern, as shown
at left. This helps the plants spread efficiently and gives the bed
a neat, natural look as the ground cover fills in.

Right: These acid-stained concrete steps have a pleasantly mottled, marblelike appearance. Below: Short stone walls line the edges of this stone walkway to separate the path from plantings.

Walkways and steps can be as beautiful as they are functional. Though their primary purpose is to provide easy and safe passage across a yard, they can be extremely effective at setting a tone, creating a sense of anticipation for guests, and introducing interesting detail to the front yard.

Many materials can be used, from classics such as brick and stone to newer options such as decorative concrete and interlocking pavers. All are very serviceable; the decision is usually one of cost, ease of installation, and general aesthetics. Visit a masonry yard or stone yard to see a wide selection of available materials.

Brick Brick has long been a popular choice for walkways because of its natural look and its modular shape, which makes it easy to work with. Brick is not as strong and weather-resistant as concrete, but if you choose the right type, a brick walkway can last for decades with very little maintenance. Be sure to buy bricks strong enough for paving. Use bricks rated SX if your ground freezes. (MX-rated bricks are suitable only in warm climates.)

Brick pavers can be installed on a bed of gravel and sand (see page 152), or they can be mortared together on a stable concrete slab. If you are not experienced at this type of work, you may want to have it done by a masonry contractor.

Concrete pavers Today's concrete pavers are dense and tough enough to withstand heavy use and the elements. They are available everywhere in a variety of types. Inexpensive concrete pavers resemble brick, tile, or stone and can be installed like bricks or, with the interlocking types, without joints to form a surface that is smooth, solid, and suitable for heavy traffic.

Poured concrete Poured-concrete walkways are very conventional. To spruce up their curb appeal, you can opt for decorative concrete treatments (see page 180).

Natural stone Stone can be expensive, but it blends beautifully with any landscape. Marble and granite are the hardest stones. Sandstone and limestone, as well as other sedimentary stones, are more porous.

Flagstone is a general term that refers to any large, flat stone 1 to 4 inches thick. Stone yards offer various types of flagstone in shades of gray, tan, and brownish red and a variety of surface textures. Quartzite and some slates can be slippery in frosty weather.

You can place flagstone on top of stable soil to create a path quickly, or you can set flagstone in a bed of sand for greater stability (see page 150). In either case, fill the joints with your choice of plants, sand, or fine gravel.

Tile A great way to dress up concrete is to give it a tile surface. Any outdoor paving tile will work, including stone tile—just be sure to avoid materials and finishes that will be slippery when wet. The concrete must be smooth. Apply a latex bonding agent, and then set the tiles in a bed of latex-reinforced mortar. After the mortar hardens, push latex-reinforced sanded grout between the tiles, and sponge it until it is smooth.

Step Design

Steps should be at least 2 feet wide—wider if you want two people to walk abreast. Inviting steps rise gradually and have broad treads. A typical rise from one step to the next is 5 to 6 inches; treads should be 13 to 16 inches.

Top: Gray and brown ashlar stones form stairs and walls that rise elegantly to the front door.
Above: Brick pavers give a walkway a traditional look.

Left: Interlocking concrete pavers in variegated colors flow gracefully through this home's front garden.

Project: Laying a Flagstone Path

Elegantly simple, this pathway is made from flagstones set on a bed of sand and surrounded with gravel.

Unless the style of your home and garden is extremely classical, formal, or symmetrical, a curvaceous flagstone-and-gravel walkway can be the perfect path to your front door. At once casual and elegant, the mosaic look of this pathway adds a richness to the landscape while appearing to be a natural part of it.

Because flagstone is irregularly shaped, it can be used to create any number of designs. The most pleasing, however, result when the stones are carefully trimmed and fitted.

Start by outlining the path with powdered limestone or gypsum. Lay out the stones and shift them around until you achieve a design that you like and that requires the least amount of cutting or trimming. Remove the loose stones and set them to the side, maintaining the pattern.

Use a mason's hammer, a brick set, a portable saw with a masonry blade, or a portable grinder fitted with a 4½-inch diamond wheel to cut and shape the stones (be sure to wear safety glasses).

Excavate the soil to a depth of 4 inches, and then tamp the surface to firm it. To install benderboard edging, drive stakes the desired height of the benderboard at 2- to 4-foot intervals along the pathway and then screw the benderboard to them.

TIP: When installing ⅜-by-6-inch redwood benderboard edging, soak it in water, if necessary, to make it more flexible.

1 Roll out landscape fabric on the path to suppress weeds, and then tuck the edges firmly under the benderboard.

2 Pour a 2-inch-thick layer of sand over the fabric, and rake the sand smooth. If soil in your region freezes, lay down 4 inches of gravel first.

3 As you rake, moisten the sand with a fine spray of water. Take care not to disturb or saturate the sand.

4 Firm the sand using a hand tamper or a drum roller. Make several passes over the moist sand to pack it down.

5 Arrange the flagstones on the sand, and wiggle them in until they are firmly embedded while periodically checking for level.

6 Fill the spaces between the stones with gravel. To help hold the stones in place, use something small, such as decomposed granite.

Project: Laying a Brick Walkway

BEFORE & AFTER This brick-in-sand walkway transformed what was once a hodgepodge of concrete pavers (above) into a rustic, handsome entry.

One of the most classically handsome and versatile of masonry materials, brick is at home in almost any landscape and complements most home styles. Today, brick comes in an array of colorations, shapes, and sizes—including used and faux versions.

With careful preparation, a brick-in-sand walkway can be as durable as bricks set in mortar, and, of course, installation is much less labor-intensive. In addition, if you decide to change the surface down the road, you can remove the bricks in perfect condition.

The pathway shown here was in need of some serious design help: The concrete walk cut off abruptly, and the straggling concrete pavers looked like an afterthought. The new brick pathway emphasizes the balance and symmetry in the garden and is the perfect entrance to the new gate.

For a pathway that can last for decades, a mortared brick border is essential to help hold the bricks together and contain the sand. Before building the forms for a mortared brick border, excavate the path area to a depth of 4 inches.

TIP: Ease the task of carrying bricks by renting or buying a pair of brick tongs, available at masonry yards and tool rental suppliers.

1 Construct the forms from 2-by-4 lumber, and put 1-by-2 stakes along the outside edges to hold the boards in place. Support rebar down the middle on stones or blocks. Mix the concrete, and then shovel it into the forms.

2 Level the concrete by moving a screed along the tops of the forms in a sawing motion. To cure the concrete, keep it damp and covered with plastic sheeting for 3 to 7 days. When the concrete is set, remove the forms.

3 Run a mason's line along the border's outside edge to aid in alignment. Wet the bricks, mix the mortar, and spread a ½-inch-thick layer over the concrete. "Butter" the end of each succeeding brick, and join it to the last.

4 Spread 2 inches of gravel over the path. Tamp it until it's level and firm. Top it with a 2-inch layer of dampened sand, and, to make a smooth surface for the bricks, pull a strike board between the borders.

5 Starting from one corner, set the bricks in position and lightly tap each one into place with a rubber mallet, checking for level as you go. To minimize disturbance to the sand, kneel on pieces of plywood as you work.

6 Sweep fine sand into the joints between the bricks (the coarse sand used for the base will not work as well). Wet the area with a light spray to settle the sand completely. If necessary, sweep in more sand, and dampen it again.

Outdoor Lighting

After the sun goes down, outdoor lighting brings a house to life with warmth and a welcoming atmosphere.

Exterior lighting is certainly a practical addition to the landscape. Lights that mark a set of stairs or discourage intruders make a home safer, and task lights make it possible to play after-hours croquet or put a late dinner on the barbecue. Outdoor lighting has an equally important role to play as a decorative element. For curb appeal that won't quit when the sun goes down, a house needs a lighting scheme that will highlight its best features, conceal its flaws, and create dramatic effects that aren't possible by day.

Ornamental lighting, called "accent lighting," can be used in a variety of ways. Spotlights and uplights create focal points in the landscape, calling attention to a particular feature, such as a tree or a fountain; backlights and shadow lights produce outlines and silhouettes; and grazing lights aimed parallel to the surface of an object emphasize interesting textures. An effective landscape plan generally incorporates several types of accent lighting.

When designing a lighting plan, keep in mind that decorative lighting should be used judiciously. While a few strategically placed fixtures will be flattering, too much light will make the yard look like a convenience-store parking lot. The key is to leave some areas in shadow. Think carefully about which features to highlight, and use subtle light to draw the eye through the landscape rather than illuminate the entire yard. Also consider the view from indoors—once the nighttime vista is lit, you will be able to see it through the windows.

Most outdoor lighting systems are low-voltage, operating on 12 volts. Typical systems consist of a transformer, low-voltage electrical cable, and light fixtures. The transformer steps down the 120-volt house current to 12 volts and must be plugged into an outdoor

Above: Lighting along the approach, in the landscaping, and on the porch and walls brings out this home's best features at night.

Dramatic depth, shadows, and highlights are the result of an effective overall lighting design.

electrical outlet protected with a ground fault circuit interrupter (GFCI) fitted with a plastic cover. Look for a transformer that can handle at least 25 percent more than the total number of watts needed to operate all the fixtures you have chosen to install. For example, a system consisting of six 20-watt fixtures (120 watts) and twelve 10-watt fixtures (120 watts) will need a 300-watt transformer.

Compared to home remodeling projects, exterior lighting is relatively inexpensive. A 300-watt transformer usually costs from $100 to $200, although you can pay more for models that include timers and other extras. For direct-burial lighting cable, which connects the transformer to individual fixtures, or to a series of fixtures, you'll typically pay a few hundred dollars—though the price can add-up significantly if you choose ornate or specialty fixtures.

From a design standpoint, it is always safe to select simple, low-to-the-ground fixtures that will disappear into the landscape. For a bolder look, you can choose taller, more ornate lamps in an array of styles and finishes, from basic black to verdigris copper. If you opt for fixtures that will call attention to themselves, be sure to match them to your home's architectural style. For example, a Colonial house will look best with formal fixtures, while Mission-style lanterns will complement a Craftsman bungalow. If you already have exterior light fixtures attached to your house or garage, buy new fixtures in that same style.

Installing exterior lighting is often a manageable job for a do-it-yourselfer, provided that there is an existing outdoor power source. If your project calls for extensive electrical work, or if you're planning an unusually elaborate lighting scheme, you may want to hire a landscape architect to design a plan, as well as a contractor or electrician to do the installation.

Typical outdoor lighting components include a streetlight-style path light (left), a wall-mounted surface light and a ceiling-mounted downlight (top left), a solar light (above), a low-profile floodlight (top right), and four decorative styles of path lights (below).

Getting the Green Light

Nature and lights can make beautiful companions. A traditional lamp post can support flowering vines (top left) or imitate the vegetation itself, as with this gourd-shaped light (top center). Lights can hang near trees (top right), protrude from shrubs (bottom right), or wrap around tree trunks and branches (above).

Project: Installing Outdoor Lighting

These easy-to-install low-voltage pathway lights will guide visitors to the front door in style.

Pathway lighting is an extremely popular form of exterior lighting, favored because it performs a multitude of tasks: It welcomes guests, provides safe passage to and from the front door, and makes the front yard beautiful after nightfall. This project shows you how to install your own low-voltage pathway lights. (If you wish to extend conventional 120-volt wiring from the house and you are not accomplished at working with electricity, contact a licensed electrician.)

A low-voltage system is powered by a transformer, which reduces the current to a safe 12 volts. It plugs into a 120-volt exterior outlet that is protected by a ground fault circuit interrupter. The system shown here utilizes a transformer with a waterproof housing, designed for outdoor use. For more about this equipment, see page 155.

1 Place the lamps on the ground at their intended locations, and run the wire beside them. Low-voltage wire can sit on the surface or be buried. Where the wire could present a tripping hazard or be easily damaged, such as across a lawn, it should be buried.

2 Using a square-tipped shovel, remove a 12-inch-wide section of lawn along the pathway, and fold it back. Scratch a 3-inch-deep ditch in the soil for the wire. Fold the sod back in place, making a slit in it at each lamp location, and pull a loop of the wire through.

Outdoor Lighting Kits

Outdoor low-voltage lighting kits, which typically include six to 12 lights, are available at most home centers, but for a more distinctive and higher quality system, you can purchase the components individually. Kits commonly come with 14-gauge wires, but if you are planning for more than 200 watts of lighting, substitute these with 12-gauge wires to prevent lights at the end of the run from dimming.

3 Using wire strippers, strip ½ inch of insulation from the ends of two wires. Loop the stripped ends around the two terminal screws on the transformer, and tighten the screws. Plug the transformer into an outlet protected by a ground fault circuit interrupter.

4 Make the electrical connections with the transformer switched on (the low voltage presents no danger) to confirm that each lamp works. Open the connector hanging from the bottom of each lamp, and slip it over the wire. Press the connector together until it clicks into place.

Walls

A used-brick retaining wall provides the perfect backdrop for this colorful two-tiered garden.

Walls can serve a variety of purposes in a landscape plan, from providing privacy to directing foot traffic to forming a backdrop for plantings. Some walls are purely decorative, and others are essential to providing structure or retaining soil. When designed with forethought, both decorative and structural walls can add solidity and charm to a front-yard landscape.

Though most walls are made of masonry, other materials such as treated wooden railroad ties and sheet metal can be used, too. Masonry walls may be made of stone, brick, concrete, adobe, or similar materials. In some cases, walls are combined with fences (see more about fences on page 132). Consult a professional before building a wall that is more than 4 feet high or that must serve as a retaining wall.

Stone As materials go, stone is a favorite because, in a short time, it can look as though it has been in place for an eternity, especially once foliage begins to pop through cracks and crevices.

You may be able to build a wall from stones right from your own front yard—this can be a real plus both in keeping your budget low and in creating a design that looks natural in your terrain. Otherwise, visit a stone yard or building materials supplier to check out your options. Colors range from nearly pure white to shades of gray, brown, yellow, and red. Stone walls can be built with mortar or, if they are low and purely decorative, loosely laid stones.

Brick Because brick is a relatively uniform material, it is enduringly popular for building walls. As with stone, there are many types. Common brick comes rough and somewhat irregular in shape and ranges in color from light tan to deep reddish brown. Facing brick, generally regular in shape, may have a rough, decorative surface on one side. The surface of wire-cut brick has vertical strips; rough facing brick has a cracked appearance. Glazed brick has a smooth, polished side. Used brick instantly creates the look of an antique wall.

Concrete pavers Some manufacturers make interlocking concrete blocks meant for easy-

to-build retaining walls. These blocks are designed with a "batter" back, meaning they lean toward the soil that the wall is intended to retain. They come in a variety of colors and decorative faces.

Concrete blocks Walls can also be built with conventional concrete blocks, but a concrete block wall rarely looks attractive unless it is faced with stucco or stone (see page 162 for information on facing a concrete block wall with stone). Standard concrete blocks are 8 inches wide by 8 inches tall by 8 or 16 inches long.

This concrete wall has plenty of visual interest thanks to a surface of stucco that has been tooled with a pattern.

Below left: Railroad ties retain a hillside garden. Below: Wide, flat stones form a wall that appears to be centuries old.

Project: Facing a Concrete Wall

This concrete retaining wall took on a far more refined look when it was faced with stone.

One of the best ways to dress up a dull or otherwise undistinguished concrete or block wall is to cover it with a veneer of flagstones. Select the lightest and thinnest flagstones you can find—ideally, stones that are predominantly flat on one side. Irregularly shaped stones will create a natural look, while stones that are somewhat squared off will provide a geometric appearance. Choose the style that fits best with your home's architecture.

The wall should be in good condition. To remove oil stains, apply commercial concrete cleaner and scrub the spots with a stiff brush. Scrape off efflorescence, a white powdery film caused by prolonged exposure to moisture, with a wire brush when the wall is completely dry, and then clean the wall with detergent.

TIP: To clean smears or a general haze, use a solution of 10 percent muriatic acid.

1 Lay down a sheet of plywood equal in width to the wall's height next to the wall. Lay the flagstones on the plywood, arranging them to create an integrated design that will require minimal cutting and trimming.

2 Paint a coat of latex bonding agent on the wall. Mix a batch of mortar according to the instructions. Using a straight trowel, apply a ⅜-inch-thick layer of mortar to the wall (slightly thicker if the stones are not flat).

3 Starting at the bottom of the wall, press the flagstones into the mortar. Use wood shims to hold them in place and maintain consistent spacing. If adjustments are needed, make them before the mortar begins to harden.

4 Continue up to the top of the wall. Every 10 minutes or so, pull a stone from the wall to make sure at least three-quarters of its thickness is embedded in the mortar. If not, butter the back of the stone before replacing it.

5 After the mortar has hardened, slip and press additional mortar into the joints using a pointed trowel or a mortar bag. Wipe the edges with a damp towel. When the mortar begins to stiffen, strike and brush the joints.

6 On the top of the wall, install stones large enough to overhang both edges by about an inch. When the mortar has begun to harden, wash the wall with water, scrub it with a brush, and then wipe it with a wet towel.

Project: Building a Brick Wall

Brick is an outstanding material for building walls—a natural for turning corners and stepping to follow contours.

A building block of rustic, yet classical charm, brick is an ideal material for many front-yard hardscapes. Because most walls generally do not receive much wear and tear, a meticulously constructed brick wall can last through generations of home owners—and look better and better with each passing year.

Brick is also easy to handle. The units are comfortable to lift with one hand, and bricklaying takes on a certain satisfying rhythm as the job progresses.

Brick walls can be built in many different patterns. The one shown here is called "running bond." With this method, best used only for low walls, you simply stagger the units from course to course.

A brick wall must be set on a flat, level concrete footing. Dig a trench the width of the desired wall and to a depth below the frost line for your area. Level and tamp the bottom, shovel in gravel to just below the frost line, fill the trench with concrete, and then screed the surface flat and smooth. Depending on the height of the finished wall, you may need to add reinforcing bar to the trench—it's best to check with your local building department. Cover the concrete with plastic, and let it cure for two days.

Several hours before you're ready to start building, lay the bricks alongside the footing and hose them down.

TIP: If you have a lot of cutting to do, rent a diamond-bladed wet saw for a day or two.

1 Mark the outer edges of the wall on the footing. Lay the bricks down, leaving ½ inch for the joints (½-inch dowels make good spacers). Then remove the bricks from the footing.

2 Spread mortar on the footing, and lay the first brick. Apply mortar to one end of the second brick, set it in place, and continue on, checking for level.

Cutting Bricks by Hand

Place the brick on a flat, resilient surface, such as a bed of sand. Hold a brickset chisel firmly in place, and tap it with a hammer to score a cutting line on all four sides. Hold the brickset against the scored line with its bevel facing toward the piece you are eliminating. Whack the brickset hard to break the brick.

3 Cut two bricks to three-quarter length to begin the second, or header, course, and mortar the pieces in place. Then lay four headers width-wise.

4 Continue laying bricks until the wall end, or lead, is 7 or 8 bricks high and looks like stair steps. Then build the lead at the other end of the wall.

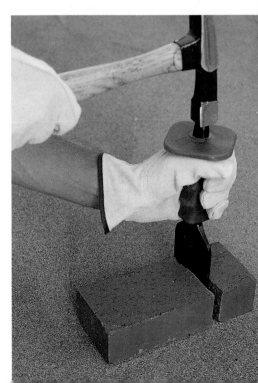

5 Stretch mason's twine between the leads. Lay bricks from the ends to the center. Apply mortar to both ends of the closure bricks, and insert them.

6 Strike the mortar joints with a finishing tool every 10 minutes or so. Smooth all of the horizontal joints first, and then smooth the vertical joints.

Trellises & Arbors

Through an archway
of vines, twin rows of
tightly groomed hedges
lead to this home's entry,
where an arbor crowns
the front door.

Arbors and trellises are great for creating a sense of entry, adding visual depth, ensuring privacy, shaping a view, providing screening, and imbuing your property with style and character. These vertical structures can have a look that is classic, contemporary, or fanciful. And, though most are made from wood, they can be made from a range of materials, including vinyl and steel.

What is the difference between a trellis and an arbor? A trellis is generally a flat framework designed to support vines. Arbors add a third dimension. In its simplest form, an arbor has two parallel trellis walls and a third trellis as a roof, which is curved in the case of a classic arched arbor. With another variation—the bower—the trellises are spread apart and built-in benches are added. A heavier, longer arbor laid out in a colonnade fashion is called a pergola.

The style of an arbor should be in keeping with the home's architecture and landscaping. An arched entry arbor, perhaps joined by a matching gate and white picket fence, offers a traditional touch. A rustic, flat-roofed structure is more appropriate for a ranch home. Regardless of the style, an arbor should be at least 7 feet tall and 5 feet wide for easy traffic flow.

Fences and walls provide ready-made backdrops for trellises—just be sure to float the supports a few inches away from wood fencing and siding to allow air space and room for plants to grow. When placing trellises near house siding, be aware that some vines can aggressively attach themselves and become a serious maintenance problem.

You can buy an arbor ready-made or as a kit, have one custom built, or build one yourself (see page 168). You may find just what you want in one of the new handcrafted trellises available through garden retailers and mail-order catalogs. Some sources carry an impressive array of trellises and arbors—from hand-forged metal types to woven wood models—that are as much a garden focal point as a support for plants. Most trellises come ready to install; arbors generally need some assembly.

Some kit gazebo manufacturers also offer large arbors, pergolas, and similar structures. You can locate these manufacturers through major home improvement centers or by searching kit gazebos on the Internet.

The surest way to attain an arbor that will add distinction and character in keeping with your home's architecture is to have one designed by a landscape designer or architect and built by a carpenter or landscape contractor (or, in the case of a metal design, a metal fabricator). For more about working with professionals, see page 102.

Above: A living arbor of crimson roses engulfs a metal trellis in this lush cottage garden.

An arbor can be part of the house, as evidenced by this heavily planted front-porch structure.

Project: Building an Arbor

This rose-filled arbor is the perfect focal point for a classic white picket fence.

Few garden structures evoke traditional suburban life like an arbor does, particularly an arbor paired with a classic picket fence. As a front-yard gateway framed in a lush climbing plant, an arbor provides the perfect complement to a cottage-style house or gives character to a home with otherwise subtle or nondescript exterior features.

The arbor shown here features a pair of broad arches that are set atop 4-by-4 posts. A series of 1-by-4 crosspieces connects the arches, forming a curved "ladder" to support blooming roses that grow abundantly up and over the arbor.

Because of the number of cuts required, a power miter saw, jig saw, and circular saw are extremely helpful tools.

Each arch is made from two layers of four 1-by-4 pieces whose ends are cut at 22½-degree angles and butted together to form a rough curve. The joints between the pieces used for the two layers are staggered to reinforce the structure—an important consideration when it comes to supporting the weight of certain plantings. One layer extends past the ends of the arch to lap the straight sections, and, at the other end, one layer laps the posts.

The posts are cut to 10 feet, and 30 inches of their length is set in concrete below ground level (for instructions on setting posts, see page 137).

All wood pieces can be primed and painted with quality exterior products before assembly. White is the traditional look for this type of arbor—and it matches the picket fence—but other neutral shades, such as light gray or tan, can be handsome when they go with the exterior house colors or complement the colors of plantings.

1 On a piece of plywood, make a mark for the center of the arch. With a pencil tied to a string, draw the curves from that point. The length of the string should be 21 inches for the inside curve and 24½ inches for the outside curve. Divide the arch into sections by marking a line down the center and then two lines 45 degrees from the center line on either side.

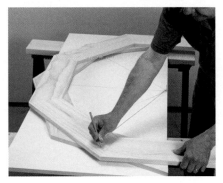

2 Cut the sections with a power miter saw, and glue them together with weatherproof glue in a staggered pattern. When the glue is dry, draw the curves on each arch assembly in the same way you created the pattern on the plywood. Extend the curved lines on the plywood into straight lines to follow where the arches will meet the straight leg sections and the posts.

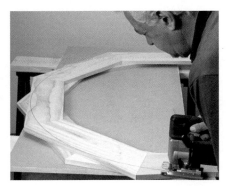

3 Cut out the arches with a jig saw, and sand the edges. Measure how far the second layer extends past the first layer, and subtract this figure from 41 inches. Cut two pieces for the straight sections to that length and two other pieces to 41 inches. Each arch will have two long straight pieces and two short straight pieces that should align when assembled.

4 Using weatherproof glue and #6-by-1¼-inch rust-resistant screws, match up the arch pieces, and then glue and screw them together. Glue and screw the short pieces to the 41-inch pieces so they are flush at the end and along the sides. Glue and screw these straight sections to the legs of the arches so the straight sections lap the arch ends.

5 Using a circular saw, cut the posts to length. Make a 1½-by-12-inch notch in one end of each post. Set two posts 42 inches apart and the other two posts 23 inches apart. Check for plumb and level, and then backfill the holes. Using weatherproof glue and #8-by-2-inch rust-resistant screws, glue and screw the arches to the posts.

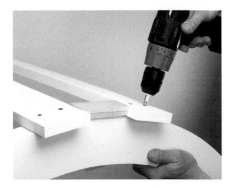

6 Starting at the center of the arch top, fasten each crosspiece with #8-by-2-inch screws, placing two at each end into predrilled holes to prevent the wood from splitting. Cut a 4-inch spacer from scrap, and use it to space the crosspieces evenly down the sides of the structure. When all crosspieces are in place, fill the screw holes with wood epoxy.

Front-Yard Gardens

A bountiful planting of perennials makes an ideal front border for many home styles.

If you want to make an impressive change to your front yard's style, you may not have to look any farther than your landscaping. A beautifully planted front yard can transform a humdrum house into something special. Coupled with a well-done facade, an attractive yard can be a showstopper.

Rehabbing the front garden can seem like a daunting prospect. If you need to do major work—regrade the plot; provide drainage; and take out or install large trees, walls, walkways, or fencing—you should consider hiring a landscape architect or, at the very least, visiting a knowledgeable and respected nursery. Professionals will understand how to showcase the best in your architecture and will establish a consistent and harmonious planting scheme tailored to your site and its conditions. Landscaping, however, is not cheap. If your budget is strict, you may want to tackle some or all of the work yourself. You will need a plan, the proper tools, and some patience because it likely will take a bit of time to accomplish.

Basic landscape design is built on several principles: balance, proportion, harmony, and diversity. Visually, landscaping should work off a focal point, usually the entry, with the areas at both sides having comparable masses of plantings or mirrored forms. The plantings should be in scale with each other as well as with the house. They should also blend seamlessly together, include enough variety to be interesting, and complement the house's architectural style. Plantings should be neither skimpy nor overwhelming.

One of the easiest ways to begin a garden design is to determine how formal you want your front yard to be. Some symmetrical architectural types, such as Federal or Greek Revival, stylistically require a formal yard with symmetrical plantings. A country cottage or ranch-style house would look odd with a formal garden but comfortable with a casual, natural, asymmetrical look. In the same way, a Spanish or Mediterranean hacienda would look as silly with a blowsy English garden as a saltbox would look with a yard full of cactus. Understanding the

Above: A rustic xeriscape garden not only saves on water but is also well suited to a contemporary architectural style.

A stately home deserves a stately garden, such as this sculpted formal bed and border of rose bushes.

Above: A trellis adorned with hanging vines or climbing plants is a hallmark of many Mediterranean-style homes.

demands of your architecture will help you get started on your garden scheme. Books and magazines devoted to a particular style will be helpful, and you may profit from some neighborhood cruising to see what others have done with similar houses.

You may also divide up the task by thinking of foundation plantings—those lining the house's foundation—and ancillary beds. With a few exceptions, a broad shrub, tree, and flower bed visible from the street and the front windows is a good choice. Compare that look to meager, narrow bands of misshapen, skimpy bushes sitting in plain patches of dirt, and you will quickly understand the appeal. The beds should be built around perennials for ease of care, with room for seasonal annuals to brighten the look. While some height is necessary to balance out the bed, windows should not disappear behind too much foliage.

Look for plants that flower at different times of the year, and, in cold-winter climates, make sure that at least some of the plants retain leaves in winter. Make sure that

The classic cottage garden is achieved by planting a profusion of old-fashioned flowers, such as sweet pea.

your selected plants share the same soil type (acid or alkaline), watering, and shade or sun requirements. For a formal look, the plantings should mirror each side of the focal point and be set in straight-line beds. For a more casual take, add gentle sweeps and curves to the beds, making one a bit deeper than the other for interest.

While you should use similar plants on either side of the focal point, you can arrange them differently and vary the quantity as long as they visually balance each other in mass, shape, and color. In formal or casual beds, an interplay of textures adds depth and complexity to the design—unless the design scheme, particularly for modern houses, is built on strict uniformity, which has its own unique appeal.

Ancillary beds include plantings on either side of walkways and between walkway pavers; front borders that parallel the sidewalk, run along the property's perimeter walls, or traverse open fencing; and freeform island beds carved into lawn or ground cover. You can choose monochrome schemes, a variety of foliage plants, or masses of flowering plants and shrubs. Again, keep the plantings consistent in mass and color to give a uniform look to all the beds,

and include some of the plants used against the foundation to unify the design. You may want to encircle a mature tree with a shade-garden bed because lawns will not grow well under deep shade. You can plant with all perennials or all annuals, but a mix of the two will ensure flowers from spring until fall.

Planting styles can be a true personal expression and a wonderful creative act. You may, for example, plant an all-white border against a dark-hued house, surround a modern house with identical tall grasses, or set a row of fluffy iceberg roses against a perfectly manicured green privet. You can play with themes, making the journey to your front door seem like a stroll through a woodland forest, a walk in the Sonoran desert, a trip to the tropics, or a venture through an exuberant English garden.

You can, and should, play textures, shapes, sizes, and colors against each other for best effect. Also consider breaking up planted borders with the occasional beautiful pot filled with overflowing plants, or add some garden ornaments such as a birdbath or garden sculpture. If you develop your design scheme carefully, plant well, and yank out any mistakes, you will soon have a front garden that is the talk of the neighborhood.

A tropical garden, with its lush, exuberant foliage, is the perfect complement to this plantation-style home.

Project: Planting a Front Border

Before planting, experiment with different arrangements until you find the one that makes you—and your plants—happiest.

Because the short trip from public space to private entry creates the first—and likely most lasting—impression visitors will have of your property, any beds that flank the walkway or border the house must be well tended. Overgrown, ill-pruned, or just up-and-dying plants send a message that the structure beyond may be receiving the same level of attention. It's no wonder that a manicured landscape rates second (after a new paint job) on the list of features that enhance the salability of a home.

If gardening is neither a talent nor an interest, there's still hope. Many attractive border designs employ hardy shrubs, grasses, and perennials that will tolerate irregular watering and fertilizing and even moderate trampling by pets. The key is to make informed plant choices and prepare the bed well. Both tasks are essential, and you will be repaid with a relatively carefree landscape.

If, on the other hand, gardening is a passion, the sky is the limit in terms of design and plant choices. Annuals require diligent fertilizing and watering, plus prompt removal and replacement when their season is over, but they can introduce a rainbow of hues year-round. Rose bushes require annual pruning and fertilizing, or they quickly become gangly and disease- and pest-ridden, but the rewards in fragrance and eye-popping color are worth the effort.

Whichever plants you choose, maintenance will be a relative snap if requirements are compatible among plants. Consider what soil amendments, fertilizers, watering schedules, and sun exposures the plants will need. In addition, pay attention to plants' space requirements at maturity; overcrowding will not only make the bed an eyesore but will also kill off the less hardy plants.

Always look for the freshest plants—ask the nursery when new plants are delivered—and resist buying those that are in full bloom. Younger plants with good leaf color that have not had a chance to become root-bound will perform better in the long run. Many smaller plants are sold as seedlings in small containers, usually six to a container in so-called "six-packs." Larger plants are sold in 1-gallon and 5-gallon containers. When

you have made your selections, arrange them in their containers on the planting bed until you are pleased with the design.

To prepare the bed for planting, dig the soil when it is neither too wet nor too dry. Soil that is too wet will make it difficult to work in amendments and will suffocate young roots. If the soil is too dry, simply water the area evenly and thoroughly. An easy test for determining optimal saturation is to squeeze some soil in your hand; the soil should form a ball that crumbles apart yet still feels moist.

As you dig, break up the soil and sift out any debris. When you have dug down 8 to 12 inches, spread the soil amendments over the surface and double-dig them in—turn the soil in one direction and again in the opposite direction—so that soil and amendments are well incorporated. You are now ready to set your plants in the bed.

Planting Container Plants

1 Dig a hole twice the width of the plant's root ball. Fill the hole with water and, after the water drains, refill it. If the second filling drains in an hour or less, drainage is good.

2 Set the plant container in the hole. Lay a shovel handle across the hole at the height of the root ball. One-gallon plants should sit about ½ inch above grade.

3 Holding the plant gently by its stem, turn the container over and tap the bottom until the plant is released. Spread out any tightly knit roots, and set the plant in the hole.

4 Fill the hole halfway with the dug-out soil, and then fill the hole halfway with water. Check the elevation of the root ball, finish backfilling the hole with soil, and then water again.

Project: Pruning

When it comes to plant health and appearance, less is more, as this well-pruned border attests.

No matter how beautiful the house is, a front yard filled with overgrown trees, bushes, and hedges visually diminishes a property. Pruning is more than mere housekeeping, however. You can prune to open up a view, maintain the proper proportion of landscaping to house, help natural light reach the house, and provide safe passage along walkways. Keeping front-yard landscaping in good order may seem like a daunting task, but you can handle smaller trees, shrubs, and hedges without much trouble if you have the proper tools, some basic pruning know-how, and a good eye. To handle the pruning of tall, mature trees safely, bring in professionals with the proper equipment.

High-quality pruning tools can make tough jobs easy and are worth the extra investment. For trees and shrubs, you will want a pair of hand shears to take care of smaller jobs; anvil or long-handled hook-and-blade loppers for small branches; and a curved, straight, or bow-frame saw for bigger branches. For hedges, you will need either handheld shears or an electric trimmer. Pole saws are used for very high, heavy branches—they should be used with extreme care. When pruning overhead, use goggles, and consider wearing a hard hat.

Every tree and shrub has its own pruning needs. Some, particularly hedge plants, must be pruned quite frequently to maintain their shape. Mature trees need only occasional pruning. The goal of all pruning is to foster well-spaced, well-balanced limbs that grow outward from the trunk of the plant. All pruning jobs begin by removing broken or diseased limbs, suckers, and any branches crossing other branches or growing inward. After that, the tasks differ depending on the need.

The most common tree pruning jobs are:
■ Crown lifting, also called "limbing up"—the gradual removal of lower limbs on trees at least several years in the ground.
■ Crown thinning—opening up the tree and letting in light.
■ Crown reduction—trimming the height or width of a tree to avoid power lines or to open up a view.

After pruning, the crown (branches and foliage) should still be at least two-thirds of the tree's total height. Never simply top a tree, or, even worse, cut all branches down to the trunk—you will have ruined one of your property's most valuable natural assets.

Prune branches at an angle that matches the limb's angle to the trunk. Make the cut just outside the branch collar—the ridge, bulge, or wrinkle at the limb's base, where it joins the trunk or other branches. The branch collar contains nutrients that help it to heal well and combat the spread of decay into the trunk.

Shrub styles have evolved from tightly trimmed squares or balls to more natural looks. Hand shears work well to manicure shrubs without detracting from their natural shape. Always prune back to some active growth point—a bud or another branch, for example. Some shrubs, particularly camellias, can be pruned into sculptural small trees by limbing up the lower branches and pruning interior branches to clean up and expose the trunks. Hedges can be left naturally shaped as long as there is some uniformity to their height and spread, but when closely sheared to mimic walls, they still make attractive formal borders. If formal is your preference, be sure to shear the hedges frequently, or they will quickly look disheveled.

The time to prune depends upon the plant and your climate zone. Pruning generally is best done during the dormant season—late winter to early spring in cold-weather zones and midwinter in mild-winter areas. Check with a local nursery if you are unsure about the right time for your area.

1 Determine which shrubs need thinning to remain vigorous and have abundant blooms in the spring.

2 Cut out the oldest and weakest stems at their base after the shrub has completely finished flowering.

3 Remove the least productive canes every year to ensure greater and longer flower production.

Driveway Improvements

A gridwork of exposed aggregate and brick does double duty as a parking pad and entry patio.

The driveway is typically one of the home's most dominating front-yard features. As a result, the driveway's appearance has a significant impact on the initial impression the house gives to visitors and passersby. Just as a beautiful brick driveway can add elegance and style to a home, a shoddy or poorly maintained driveway can severely compromise an otherwise attractive property.

Driveway improvements run the gamut from stain removal and simple repairs to makeovers and entire replacements. Home owners can handle many simple repairs themselves at a minimal expense; major driveway treatments or new driveways call for a professional concrete or driveway contractor.

If your driveway needs only minor repairs—or if you're not ready to take on the expense of a major makeover—there are several things you can do to spruce it up.

Asphalt Driveways

Repair small cracks in asphalt driveways by first sweeping dirt from the cracks and then applying asphalt-repair compound with a caulking gun. Follow the compound's label directions.

To repair large cracks in asphalt, brush and remove debris with a shop vacuum. Patch holes and cracks with cold-process asphalt-repair compound, available at home improvement centers. Follow the manufacturer's directions.

You can clean an asphalt driveway by scrubbing it with a solution of detergent and water (use a stiff-bristle push broom) and then hosing it off.

If the blacktop surface of your asphalt looks dull and faded, you can improve its appearance by seal-coating it. Driveway sealers roll on much like paint and leave the driveway with the shiny black look of a completely new surface. This coating also fills in hairline cracks to seal out moisture, blocks damaging sunlight, and helps repel stains.

Concrete & Brick Driveways

To repair narrow cracks in concrete, apply concrete-patching compound with a caulking gun according to the compound manufacturer's directions. If a crack is wider than ¼ inch, use a cold chisel and mason's hammer to widen and undercut the crack (wear safety glasses). Brush out loose debris, and then apply concrete-patching compound with a trowel, completely filling the void. After the patching compound begins to set, wet the trowel, and use it to smooth out the patch so it is flush with the slab. Keep the patch slightly damp for about a week to allow the concrete to cure slowly.

Concrete and brick driveways can be cleaned with a power washer and coated with a clear masonry sealer. Certain types of stains require a bit more effort.

Oil and grease stains can usually be lightened if not entirely removed. Scatter fine sawdust, cat litter, cement powder, or hydrated lime over the surface to soak up as much of the oil or grease as possible, and then sweep up the residue. If an older stain has penetrated, try dissolving it with a commercial degreaser or emulsifier. You can also attempt to lighten residual stains with bleach. Scrub in a 1:4 bleach-water solution, let it stand, and then rinse the surface. Repeat if necessary. Be sure to wear rubber gloves, safety glasses, and old clothes when working with bleach.

Driveway Makeovers

If your driveway is beyond repair, maybe a facelift is in order. Repaving a standard asphalt driveway is one option. But if you really want to transform your driveway, consider another surface or a combination of materials. Many of the same paving materials used for patio surfaces—including brick, stone, and loose materials such as gravel—

Filling a Crack

Narrow cracks in concrete can be repaired quickly with special masonry repair caulk.

Patching a Large Crack

1 Use a cold chisel and mason's hammer to break away loose concrete and widen the crack below the surface. Brush out debris.

2 Fill the crack with concrete-patching compound, using a brick trowel to stuff the patch into the crack. Scrape the patch level.

TIP: To prevent surface defects such as hairline cracks and flaking from becoming worse, apply concrete sealer.

Handsome and practical, this driveway has a center strip of loose pebbles and stones flanked by two slabs of stained concrete.

work well for driveways. These can make a driveway seem less one-dimensional and utilitarian even if its true function hasn't changed. The extra expense will almost always increase the property's value.

Although concrete is a bit more expensive than asphalt, concrete is more durable and can be stained or finished in numerous ways (see below). Brick can be set in a variety of patterns; there is nothing like brick to enhance a formal setting, but it's costly. (See more about types of brick on page 161.)

Decorative Effects for Concrete

A concrete driveway need not be that expansive river of gray typical to so many homes. A number of techniques exist today that add color and texture to both new and old poured concrete driveways. Because creating a custom driveway is generally a large and exacting undertaking, it is best left to professionals.

Following is a sampling of popular treatments and what to look for in a quality job.

Seeding aggregate Composed of attractive pebbles or small stones, seed aggregate is applied by a shovel in a single layer right after the bleed water (water that rises to the surface) from a newly poured concrete driveway has evaporated. Then a float is used to press the stones down until they lie just below the surface. When the slab begins to harden, a fine mist of water is lightly applied, and the aggregate is swept to expose the surface of the stones. Only the tops of the stones should be exposed—any more and the stones could later come loose. Muriatic acid is used to remove any residual surface haze.

Coloring New concrete may be colored in one of two ways, both using dry concrete colorant. The most reliable method is to have the colorant added to the dry concrete ingredients before the water is added to the mix. The other is to have the colorant dusted on the concrete before it has set. With the latter, about two-thirds of the recommended amount of colorant is sifted onto the concrete, and the surface is floated. Then the remaining colorant is applied, the surface is floated again, and finally, the surface is finished with a steel trowel or broom.

Staining If your driveway is in good repair, you can give it a real facelift and even achieve the look of travertine or marble by staining it. Most driveways must first be cleaned to remove any surface oil or grease. Then a special cleaner containing acid is applied to make the concrete porous enough to absorb the stain. In addition to stone-like trompe l'oeil looks, you can also create the same faux finishes that you could apply to a wall using brushes and sponges. Ask your contractor to show you samples of the various effects that you can achieve.

Stamping and tooling Stamping and tooling are faux treatments that make concrete surfaces appear to be flagstones or other

This concrete driveway was stained and engraved to look like stone.

types of pavers. They require pouring a new concrete driveway or coating an aging one with a ½-inch-thick layer of polymer-enhanced concrete, stamping it with a special stamping tool, and staining it to create the desired look. The indentations are made after the concrete is poured but before it has set, so it is advisable to be on-site to help oversee the design during this process. It is also a good idea to create something of a pattern beforehand so that you can show your concrete contractor the kind of effect you are trying to achieve.

Engraving or cutting patterns Special tools are used for engraving concrete, usually to create a shallow series of meandering grooves that appear to be grout lines. On large driveways, engraving adds texture and interest and breaks up the material's monotony.

A concrete saw and a straightedge are the only tools required to cut patterns—an effect similar to, though less subtle than, engraving. With these tools, a concrete slab (often stained first) can be divided into geometric sections or be segmented into random areas. Staining or painting the sections in contrasting colors after cutting can create a range of looks, from dramatic to playful.

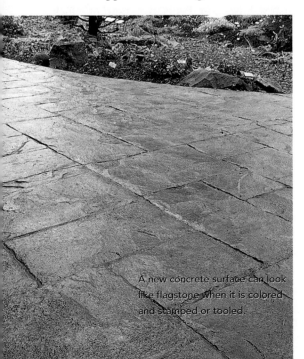

A new concrete surface can look like flagstone when it is colored and stamped or tooled.

New Driveways

A new driveway can be an elegant design element and provide ample parking and improved access to the house. But before embarking on a new driveway project, give some thought to the paving materials and layout.

The shape of the driveway depends upon the site and the home owners' needs. It's important to consider a number of questions: Where does your garage sit on the property, and what's the best route to it? Do you want to call attention to or downplay your driveway? Can you soften or conceal parts of it with landscaping?

If you completely redesign your driveway, make sure it is at least 10 feet wide. Also remember that curving driveways must be wide enough to accommodate a car's turning radius. The site should be clear of tree limbs and shrubbery that could scratch a car, and trees should be set back several feet to minimize the possibility of roots cracking the surface.

Think about your current driveway's overall design. Sometimes reconfiguring its path can make a tremendous difference in the way your home looks and functions.

Right: A twin set of sectional roll-up doors appears less massive than a single door for two cars.

A hinged garage door can be good looking but only works in single-car sizes and must be operated manually.

As typically one of the most prominent features of a property, the garage door is critical to appearance. And, as one of the largest moving parts of a home, the garage door must not just look good but also function well.

Unfortunately, garage doors are subjected to harsh weather and daily usage, both of which can cause them to look shoddy and perform poorly over time. If a new paint job is not enough to revive your garage door, it is probably better to replace it with a new model.

Today, garage doors come in a range of styles and materials and are easier to maintain and operate than ever before. Following is a close look at the main types available.

Most garage doors are either tilt-ups or sectional roll-ups. A sectional door, the most common type, is made up of several sections that are hinged together. It travels straight and back on rollers that move through channeled tracks along each side. A torsion spring across the top of the door or extension springs along the sides help when lifting or lowering the door. Although the latter system is easier and safer to install, a torsion spring requires less maintenance.

One-piece swing-up doors pivot up and down on hinges and are assisted by large springs on each side. Though they cost 25 percent to 35 percent less than roll-up doors, they offer less headroom, do not seal the garage opening as tightly or securely, and swing outward—which means you cannot park your car within 2 to 3 feet of them.

A third type of door—hinged—is split vertically down the middle and attaches with hinges to the side jambs of a single-car garage. This type must be operated manually and requires room to swing, but it looks less dominating and conventional than other doors.

Both roll-up and swing-up doors are made from a variety of materials in flush, raised-panel, and recessed-panel designs and can be purchased with options such as windows and electric garage door openers.

If you want to buy a door and have it installed, look up "Garage Doors & Door Operating Devices" in the Yellow Pages to find companies that distribute or manufacture and install doors. Be sure to get at least three bids. If you intend to install your own garage door, check out the offerings at home centers. Be sure the door you buy comes with complete, easy-to-follow instructions and, if it has extension springs, includes an extension-spring containment kit for safety.

Most manufacturers offer window sections that provide daylight within the garage and a decorative accent. The windows in these sections may have conventional single glazing or energy-efficient dual glazing.

A door that has an electric operator is more likely to be closed most of the time than a model without. This makes your home secure and keeps it looking tidy. Good operators have lifetime warranties, photoelectric safety devices, and frequency codes that cannot be cracked by thieves.

Garage doors are made from wood, steel, aluminum, or fiberglass. Each of these materials has its own benefits and drawbacks, although wood and steel are favored for a variety of reasons.

Wood Although wood is an affordable and attractive material, it is subject to weather damage. Variations in heat and moisture make wood expand and contract, causing it to warp over time and require periodic repainting or refinishing.

In many cases, a tilt-up wood door can be built right in the driveway by applying a skin of exterior plywood to a frame of Douglas fir, spruce, or similar softwood. Or the frame and plywood can be covered with siding to match the house, a technique that can contribute greatly to the overall appearance of a home. Unless you are an accomplished carpenter, this job is best left in the hands of a garage door installer.

Roll-up wood door sections may have either flush or panel sections. Flush types are made by fastening a plywood panel or wood-composite panel over a wooden frame. With panel construction, manufacturers fit several rectangular plywood or wood-composite panels into a wooden frame.

If you want to apply a wood stain to your garage door, choose a stain-quality door that has solid-wood panel inserts. Be aware that types constructed of panels with several pieces edge-glued together may show joints when the panels are stained.

Steel If you want a garage door that is strong, durable, and secure, choose steel. If this sounds too industrial, rest assured that, thanks to durable coatings and embossing technologies, many of the newer steel doors do a fairly successful job of imitating the look of wood. Unlike wood doors, steel doors will not crack or warp, and they have extremely durable finishes. They are often warranted against everything except fading for as long as you own the house. One drawback is that steel can dent, and the dents can be difficult to fix. High-quality steel doors are 2 inches thick and are clad in 24-gauge steel with a core of rigid foam insulation built into a steel frame.

Aluminum If your home's curb appeal is a high priority, you may not want to opt for an aluminum garage door. Though aluminum garage doors are lightweight and rustproof and are made attractive by durable finishes and wood-grain embossing, they are easily dented—and dents can be difficult to fix.

Fiberglass Translucent fiberglass doors are sometimes appropriate for corrosive ocean climates or where plenty of daylight is wanted inside the garage. But fiberglass cracks and breaks fairly easily and may yellow with age, so it may not be the right choice for improving curb appeal.

TIP: An electric garage door operator makes it easier to keep the door closed— and keep clutter out of view.

This large tilt-up garage door, made as a single panel, complements the house's siding.

Building a Recycling Center

BEFORE & AFTER Before this new recycling center was built, garbage cans and recycling bins were a real eyesore.

Do you store your trash cans, recycling bins, and garden supplies in your side yard? If you do—and that area is visible from the street—you can greatly improve your home's curb appeal by building a storage center for your trash and recycling. Such a structure can not only lend order to a jumbled mess outdoors but can also alleviate the buildup of recyclables indoors by providing dry outdoor storage.

The center shown here is designed to match the house's exterior, making the structure look like a small addition to the side of the house. This example took two weekends to construct. Finished, it is 8 feet wide by 30 inches deep by 58 inches tall. Of course, you may want to adjust these dimensions according to the sizes of your trash cans and recycling bins.

Cut a pressure-treated 2 by 4 to a length of 90 inches to serve as a ledger. To protect the house against moisture and termites, attach 6-inch-wide aluminum flashing with 1-inch roofing nails where the ledger will go. Check for level, and then attach the ledger to the house with deck screws.

Cut three 48-inch-long 2 by 4s to serve as vertical supports against the house. Attach flashing where the supports will go, and then attach the two outer supports so their edges extend 1½ inches beyond the ledger (these edges will support the end rafters). Finally, attach the third support.

If the surface of your side yard is concrete and fairly level, the structure may be able to sit right on the slab. If the surface is made of an uneven material such as brick, you will need to remove it and set the posts in concrete. (See Building a Fence on page 136 for instructions.) Trim the post tops to 46 inches above ground level.

Use two 2 by 4s, each cut to 93 inches in length, to make the top plate. Fasten them to the tops of the posts with 8d nails. Cut two 2 by 4s to 30 inches and two 2 by 4s to 28½ inches to make the rafters, and then cut the

1 Build the basic framework, attaching it to a pressure-treated 2-by-4 ledger along the house's wall.

bird's-mouth notches. Toenail the longer rafters at the ends of the top plate and the shorter rafters in the middle.

Cut seven pieces of 2 by 4 to 22¼ inches in length to make the shelf and siding supports. Check for level, and then nail them to the vertical supports and posts. Cut two shelves from a 4-by-8-foot sheet of ½-inch plywood. Cut the optional third shelf to 65 by 18 inches. Attach the shelving.

Cut a 4-by-8-foot piece of ½-inch plywood to 30 inches in width. Center it on the rafters, and then nail it in place. Also nail ½-inch plywood panels to the shelf supports.

Nail roof flashing to the plywood's edges, and staple roofing paper to the plywood's surface. Finish with the roofing material used for the roof of the house (cedar shingles in this case).

Finish both ends with cedar or redwood siding and battens. Cover the rafter fronts and sides with 3¼-by-⅝-inch cedar or redwood trim. Glue and then nail 1¼-by-¼-inch wood strips to the front edge of each shelf. Finally, paint or stain the structure to match the house.

TIP: Adjust the dimensions of this center to fit your recycling bins and garbage cans.

2 Add ½-inch plywood sheathing to the roof rafters, nailing it at the edges. Then install the plywood shelves.

3 Install siding to match the house, and flash the roof's perimeter. Paint the structure, and apply roofing.

Water Features

Right: This large, artistic spill fountain cascades water down a series of descending bowls. Below: A custom-made pedestal fountain is the perfect accent to this entry garden.

A water feature gives a house the kind of curb appeal that goes beyond good looks. Water is more than just a lovely addition to the landscape—it fills the air with pleasant sounds, attracts birds and other wildlife, and makes the garden seem cooler on a hot afternoon. Though a fountain or pool is usually a backyard fixture, when placed in the front of the house, it creates an oasis of peace that beckons visitors to step inside.

A water feature can be as large as a lagoon or as small as a salad bowl, as complicated as a waterfall or as simple as a birdbath. Buy a ready-made decorative pool or fountain from a garden store or home center, or build your own from a kit or from scratch. In the front yard, a waterscape of modest proportions is usually best. From a design point of view, it should function as an accent rather than as a focal point. For safety reasons, it should contain no more than a few inches of water unless you plan to install a secure fence (see Water Safety, opposite). It is not necessary to choose something expensive or elaborate; even an ordinary pot or bowl outfitted with a recirculating bubbler can add immeasurably to a garden's charm. On the other hand, an imposing water feature may be fine for a large front yard, provided that you take proper safety precautions.

The first step in selecting a water feature is to determine what its basic elements should be. You may want to include moving water, which produces a soothing musical murmur and masks the sound of street traffic. Or you may prefer the tranquility of still water, which creates a glassy, calm surface that reflects the beauty of the garden. You will also need to decide whether your water feature will contain fish or plants. Even a small homemade water garden fashioned from a pot can support diminutive mosquito fish and plants that thrive with their roots underwater. Moving water is best for fish because it contains extra oxygen, while a still pool makes a hospitable environment for water plants. Make sure that the style of your water feature is compatible with your existing landscape features. A fountain or pond with geometric lines will look best with a formal house and garden. A water feature that mimics shapes found in nature will complement an informal architectural style.

If you want moving water in the front yard, a portable fountain is by far the easiest and safest option. There are two basic types: spray fountains, which spurt water in a specific pattern, and spill fountains, which splash water over an ornamental fixture into a catch basin. Some are freestanding, and others must be attached to a wall. Even an inexperienced do-it-yourselfer can construct a spill fountain from a simple container, reservoir, and pump (see page 188). Most

pumps operate on 120 volts, but low-voltage (12-volt) versions make installation much less risky.

When deciding where to place your water feature, keep in mind that any type with moving water will need to be connected to a power source. If the location you have chosen will require digging up the yard to bring in electrical wiring and water pipes, consider a site that is close to the house, or think about installing a still pool that you can fill with the hose. If you are planning to grow water plants, look for a spot that gets at least 5 hours of direct sunlight a day. (Because a shallow water garden will evaporate quickly in the sun, you may want to install a float valve connected to a water supply to keep the water level steady.) A spray fountain should be protected from the wind, which will blow water about and cause it to evaporate quickly. For a water feature that requires excavation, check the location of utility lines before digging, select a level site if possible, and avoid placing a pond beneath trees, where it will catch debris. No matter what type of water feature you are installing, put it in a place that is easily viewed, and keep in mind that the water's surface will reflect its surroundings.

If you're putting in a water feature that is more than 18 inches deep or one that requires plumbing and electrical work, you may be required to obtain a permit from your local building department. Building codes may also govern how close to the property line you can put a larger water garden, and in some areas you may be required to include protective fencing.

Elegantly simple, this small Asian-style fountain spills a trickle of water through a small bamboo spout into a ceramic pot.

Water Safety

Safety is a pressing concern when you're installing a water feature in the front yard. Young children can drown in less than a foot of water, and even able-bodied adults can stumble into a pond that's flush with the ground. Because the front yard is accessible from the street, a water feature must not pose a risk to anyone.

The most prudent course of action is to choose a water feature that has no standing water, such as a fountain with a pebble-filled bottom. A fountain that sits on a pedestal or hangs on the wall above the reach of toddlers is another option. If you are intent on creating a large water feature such as a pond, it is wise to put a fence around it (in some areas, the law requires this precaution). Stores that specialize in water features also sell protective devices such as alarms and child-proof covers—but do not rely only upon these.

When constructing a large water feature, the surface surrounding it should be stable and skid-resistant. A raised pool is easier to see than a sunken one, and a shelf around the inside perimeter provides a way out of the water if someone should fall in.

Project: Making a Wall Fountain

In this courtyard garden, water gently splashes from the mouth of a terra-cotta sunburst into a shallow basin surrounded by foliage.

One of the most charming ways to welcome visitors to your home is with the soothing sound of falling water. While a large spray or spill fountain can present a hazard to children or small pets, a wall fountain with a shallow pool or basin can safely achieve the same effect without the risk. In addition, a wall fountain takes up little space, making it an ideal feature for a small front yard.

The most effective wall fountains create the illusion that water is spouting from a hidden spring. Almost any item can be used—a piece of stained glass, a gnarled driftwood branch, even an old watering can. Whatever you choose, the mechanism for all water fountains is the same: Water circulates through plastic tubing from a pool or basin containing a small pump to an outlet that returns the water to the pool or basin.

In the project shown here, a terra-cotta sunburst mask adds a touch of whimsy. Because many wall fountains, including the one shown here, are heavy, choose a size and style that can be securely attached to the surface; in this case, the brick wall can easily support the weight of the mask.

The sunburst was installed with a small 120-volt pump, but a low-voltage pump and transformer work just as well. Here, the wisteria growing up and over the wall hides the clear vinyl tubing, but any sort of vining plant or even a trellis placed against the wall will serve the same purpose. Alternatively, you can run the tubing up the back of the wall and through a hole drilled with a long masonry bit, and then attach the mask to the wall with a metal dowel and mortar.

To ensure water tightness, the interior of the basin in this example was coated with a sealing agent; a sheet of vinyl lining could also be used.

1 Place the mask face down. At each corner, glue pieces of cork to allow clearance for the plastic tubing when the mask is hung on the wall. With an electric drill and masonry bit, drill a hole at a 45-degree angle halfway through the mask above the waterspout hole.

2 Slide one end of an elbow fitting into a piece of clear vinyl tubing that is long enough to run from the mask to the basin below. Cut a second piece of tubing, connect it to the other end of the fitting, and push it through the back of the mask's waterspout hole.

TIP: Be sure a ground fault circuit interrupter (GFCI) protects the electrical outlet that serves the pump.

3 With the electric drill and masonry bit, drill a hole 1½ inches deep at a 45-degree angle into the brick wall, and slide a 3-inch-long metal dowel into it. Hang the mask on the wall by sliding the metal dowel into the hole drilled into the back of the mask.

4 Wind one end of the tubing through the vines and down the wall. Slide the other end of the tubing over the outlet of the pump, and place the pump in the basin. Fill the basin with water, and then plug the pump into a ground fault circuit interrupter outlet.

Credits

Photography

1 Norman A. Plate. **2** Jessie Walker. **3** *top* Sylvia Martin/SPC Photo Collection. **3** *middle left* SPC Photo Collection. **3** *middle right* Norman A. Plate. **3** *bottom* Tim Street-Porter. **4–5** *both* Jean Allsopp/SPC Photo Collection. **6** Derek Fell. **7** *both* Mark Luthringer. **8–10** *all* Brian Vanden Brink. **11** Doug Keister. **12** Tim Street-Porter. **13** *top* Laurey Glenn/SPC Photo Collection. **13** *bottom* Jessie Walker. **14–15** *all* Van Chaplin/SPC Photo Collection. **16** *both* Jean Allsopp/SPC Photo Collection. **17** *both* Allen Rokach/SPC Photo Collection. **18** *top* Jean Allsopp/SPC Photo Collection. **18** *bottom* Steve Bender. **19** *both* SPC Photo Collection. **20–23** *all except 21 bottom left* Van Chaplin/SPC Photo Collection. **21** *bottom left* Joel Blackstock. **24** *both* Richard Maack. **25** *all* Jean Allsopp/SPC Photo Collection. **26** *both* Dominique Vorillon. **27** *both* Weldon Brewster. **28** Brian Vanden Brink. **29** *top* Saxon Holt. **29** *bottom* Sylvia Martin/SPC Photo Collection. **30** Glenn Cormier. **31** *top* Thomas J. Story. **31** *bottom* Steven Gunther. **32** *all* Jean Allsopp/SPC Photo Collection. **33** Norman A. Plate. **34** Robert Benson. **35** Jessie Walker. **36** *top* Grey Crawford. **36** *bottom* Erik Johnson. **37** *both* Ray Kachatorian/Freshstock. **38** Janet Loughrey. **39** Steven Gunther. **40** *top* Tim Street-Porter. **40** *bottom* Brian Vanden Brink. **41** Dan Gregory. **42** *both* Doug Keister. **43** *top left* Saxon Holt. **43** *top right* Tim Street-Porter. **43** *bottom left* Brian Vanden Brink. **43** *bottom right* Saxon Holt. **44–45** *all* Brian Vanden Brink. **46** *both* Jean Allsopp/SPC Photo Collection. **47** *both* Van Chaplin/SPC Photo Collection. **48** *both* Artifex. **49** Sylvia Martin/SPC Photo Collection. **50–51** *all* Mark Luthringer. **52** *top* Thomas J. Story. **52** *bottom right* Ted Betz. **53** *both* SPC Photo Collection. **54** *both* Van Chaplin/SPC Photo Collection. **55** *all* Steven Gunther. **56** *top and bottom* Derek Fell. **56** *middle* Allen Rokach/SPC Photo Collection. **57** *top* Derek Fell. **57** *bottom* Steven Gunther. **58** *both* Lauren Springer Ogden. **59** Ben Woolsey. **60** Doug Keister. **61** Brian Vanden Brink. **62** *top left* Peter O. Whiteley. **62** *top right* Derek Fell. **62** *bottom* Brian Vanden Brink. **63** Jay Graham. **64** John Granen. **65** Brian Vanden Brink. **66** Tim Street-Porter. **67** *all except top right* Derek Fell. **67** *top right* Brian Vanden Brink. **68** *both* Jean Allsopp/SPC Photo Collection. **69** *both* Van Chaplin/SPC Photo Collection. **70** Jessie Walker. **71** *top right* Van Chaplin/SPC Photo Collection. **71** *middle left* Jean Allsopp/SPC Photo Collection. **71** *bottom right* Peter O. Whiteley. **72** *top* Tina Evans. **72** *bottom* Derek Fell. **73** *top left* www.KenRicePhoto.com. **73** *top right* Van Chaplin/SPC Photo Collection. **73** *bottom left* Tim Street-Porter. **73** *bottom right* Brian Vanden Brink. **74** *top* James Frederick Housel. **74** *bottom* www.KenRicePhoto.com. **75** *all* Peter Malinowski/In Site. **76** Norman A. Plate. **77** *top left* Allen Rokach/SPC Photo Collection. **77** *top right* Saxon Holt. **77** *bottom* Gary Conaughton. **78–79** *all* Van Chaplin/SPC Photo Collection. **80** *top* Brian Vanden Brink. **80** *bottom* www.KenRicePhoto.com. **81** *all but bottom right* Sylvia Martin/SPC Photo Collection. **81** *bottom right* Ken Chen. **82** *first bottom* Dave Newman. **82** *second top* Georgene Takayma. **82** *second middle* Bruce W. Gourley. **82** *second bottom* RunningDogStudio@cox.net. **82** *third top* Bill Fox. **82** *third upper middle* Molly Blauvelt. **82** *third lower middle* Richard Falzone. **82** *fourth top* Carol Sussman Henke. **82** *fourth middle* Amy Wellborn. **82** *fourth bottom* Natalie Sylvester. **83** Tim Street-Porter. **84** *top two* Jean Allsopp/SPC Photo Collection. **84** *bottom left* Brian Vanden Brink. **84** *bottom right* Allen Rokach/SPC Photo Collection. **85** www.BobPerron.com. **86** *top right* Saxon Holt. **86** *left* Norman A. Plate. **86** *bottom right* Saxon Holt. **87** *left* Doug Keister. **87** *right top* www.BobPerron.com. **87** *right upper middle* Sylvia Martin/SPC Photo Collection. **87** *right lower middle and bottom* Brian Vanden Brink. **88** *both* www.ArchitecturalPhotographer.com. **89** *top two* Sylvia Martin/SPC Photo Collection. **89** *bottom two* Bob Bretell. **90** *top two* Jay Graham. **90** *bottom two* Laurie Black. **91** *both* Sylvia Martin/SPC Photo Collection. **92–93** *both* Ken Chen. **94** *all* Norman A. Plate. **95** *all* Grey Crawford. **96–97** *all* Steven Gunther. **98** Tim Street-Porter. **99** *top* www.BobPerron.com. **99** *bottom* Brian Vanden Brink. **100** *left* Brian Vanden Brink. **100** *right* www.BobPerron.com. **101** *top left* Jean Allsopp/SPC Photo Collection. **101** *top right* Tim Street-Porter. **101** *bottom left* Jean-Claude Hurni. **101** *bottom right* Van Chaplin and Allen Rokach/SPC Photo Collection. **102–104** *all* Van Chaplin/SPC Photo Collection. **105** Don Vandervort. **106** Photo Courtesy of Simpson Door Co. **107** Jessie Walker. **108** *top* Photo Courtesy of Simpson Door Co. **108** *bottom* Photo Courtesy of Therma-Tru Doors. **109** *top* Photo Courtesy of Pella Corp. **109** *bottom* Derek Fell. **110** *both* Photo Courtesy of Baldwin Door Hardware. **111** *all* John Reed Forsman. **112** Photo Courtesy of Alcoa Home Exteriors Inc. **113** *both* Don Vandervort. **114** *top left* Nick Williams & Associates. **114** *top right* Photo Courtesy of Anderson Windows. **114** *bottom* Photo Courtesy of American Wood Council. **115** *both* Photo Courtesy of Anderson Windows. **116** *top* Don Vandervort. **116** *bottom* Photo Courtesy of Zappone Manufacturing. **117** Photo Courtesy of Craftsman. **118–119** *all* Eric Hanson. **120–121** *all* Photo Courtesy of Anderson Windows. **122** Photo Courtesy of Pella Corp. **123** *top* Photo Courtesy of Pella Corp. **123** *bottom* Photo Courtesy of Kolbe & Kolbe. **124** Scott Gibson. **125** *all* Geoffrey Gross. **126** Jeffrey Becom. **128** Don Vandervort. **129** Doug Keister. **130** *top* Sylvia Martin/SPC Photo Collection. **130** *bottom three* John Reed Forsman. **131** *all* John Reed Forsman. **132** Philip Harvey. **133** *top* Alan & Linda Detrick. **133** *middle* Don Vandervort. **133** *bottom* Derek Fell. **134** *top* Sylvia Martin/SPC Photo Collection. **134** *bottom left* E. Andrew McKinney. **134** *bottom right* Jamie Hadley. **135** *top* E. Andrew McKinney. **135** *bottom* Jamie Hadley. **136** *top* Allen Rokach/SPC Photo Collection. **136–137** *all except 136 top* E. Andrew McKinney. **138** SPC Photo Collection. **139** *all* E. Andrew McKinney. **140** *both* SPC Photo Collection. **141** *top* Norman A. Plate. **141** *bottom* Michael S. Thompson. **142–143** *all* SPC Photo Collection. **144** Van Chaplin/SPC Photo Collection. **145–146** *all* Norman A. Plate. **147** *top* Charles Mann. **147** *bottom* Norman A. Plate. **148** *top right* Photo Courtesy of Concrete Art. **148** *bottom left* Jerry Pavia. **149** *top* Crandall & Crandall. **149** *middle* Allan Mandell. **149** *bottom* Frank Gaglione. **150–151** *all* Norman A. Plate. **152** *left* Thomas J. Story. **152** *right* Marion Brenner. **153** *middle left and center* Marion Brenner. **153** *top, middle right, and bottom three* Norman A. Plate. **154** SPC Photo Collection. **155** *both* Photo Courtesy of Nightscaping. **156** *top seven* Cheryl Fenton. **156** *bottom four* Photo Courtesy of Nightscaping. **157** *top left and top right* SPC Photo Collection. **157** *top middle* Lynne Harrison. **157** *bottom left* Thomas J. Story. **157** *bottom right* Suzanne Woodard. **158–159** *all* Mark Roskams. **160** Marion Brenner. **161** *top* Robin B. Cushman. **161** *bottom left* Jerry Pavia. **161** *bottom right* Norm Plate. **162** Jerry Pavia. **163–165** *all* Frank Gaglione. **166** *top* Jamie Hadley. **166** *bottom* Tim Street-Porter. **167** *top* Susan A. Roth. **167** *bottom* J. Scott Smith. **168** Jean Allsopp/SPC Photo Collection. **169** *all* Roger Foley. **170** Saxon Holt. **171** *top* Tom Wyatt. **171** *bottom* Brian Vanden Brink. **172** *top* Jerry Harpur. **172** *bottom* Susan A. Roth. **173** Roger Foley. **174–175** *all* Norman A. Plate. **176–178** *all* Saxon Holt. **179** *top right* Dan Stultz. **179** *bottom two* Frank Gaglione. **180** Saxon Holt. **181** *top* Gary Conaughton. **181** *bottom* Michael S. Thompson. **182** *top* Photo courtesy of Clopay Building Products. **182** *bottom* Sylvia Martin/SPC Photo Collection. **183** Don Vandervort. **184–185** *all* Thomas J. Story. **186** *top* Charles Mann. **186** *bottom* Nick Williams & Associates. **187** Robin B. Cushman. **188–189** *all* Thomas J. Story

Design

3 *top* Designer: Tim Hilkhuijsen. **3** *bottom* Designer: Tichenor Thorpe Landscapists. **4–5** Styling: Elizabeth Harrell. **7** Designer: Chris Jacobson/GardenArt. **8** Architect: Sally Weston. **10** *bottom* Designer: Smith Alvarez Seinkiewycz Architects. **14** Designer: Fay Hurt. **16** Architect: Stephen Feller. **20–21** Designers: Joel and Laura Blackstock. **22–23** Landscape Architect: J. Dabney Peeples; Residential Designer: Jack Thacker. **25** Architect: Peter Moor. **26** Designers: Larry Brisley, Architect, and Jim Gelfat, Architect. **28** Designer: Robinson & Grisaru Architects. **29** *bottom* Architect: Sinclair Black **30** Designer: Galvin Cristilli Architects. **31** *top* Designers: Michele Maidens and Francisco Hernandez. **31** *bottom* Designer: Chris Rosmini Landscape Design. **32** Styling: Mary Lyn H. Jenkins. **34** Architect: Robert Harper. **39** Designer: Nicole Lopez. **40** *top left* Designer: Riccardo Legorreta. **40** *bottom left* Designer: Rick Burt, Architect. **40–41** Designer: Jeffrey Becom. **43** *top left* Designer: Saxon Holt. **43** *top right* Designer: Tichenor Thorpe Landscapists. **44** Designer: Scott Simons, Architect. **45** *right* Designer: Jack Silverio, Architect. **46** Styling: Buffy Hargett. **47** Architect: Bill Edwards; Landscape Architect: Dan Franklin. **48** Designer: Artifex. **49** Designer: Tim Hilkhuijsen. **50** *and* **51** *top* Designer: David Yakish, Gardenmakers. **51** *middle and bottom* Designer: Chris Jacobson/GardenArt. **52** Designer: Goodman Landscape Design. **53** Garden Designer: Tom Mannion. **55** Designer: Nicole Lopez. **56** *middle* Garden Designer: Ken Miller. **58** Designer: Lauren Springer Ogden. **62** *top left* Designer: Landscape Resource Group; Builder: Joseph Wood. **62** *top right* Designer: Ron Forest Fences. **63** Designer: Chris Jacobson and Beverly Sarjeant/GardenArt. **64** Designer: www.SundanceLandscaping.com. **65** *bottom* Designer: Ron Forest Fences. **66** Architect: Brian Murphy. **68** Designer: Philip Morris. **71** *top right* Garden Designer: Norman Kent Johnson. **71** *middle* Landscape Designers: Barbie Tafel Thomas and Mary Webb/Webb-Thomas. **71** *bottom right* Designer: Nick Williams & Associates. **72** *top left* Designers: Kent and Dana Campbell. **73** *top right* Designer: Fay Hurt. **73** *bottom left* Designer: Martyn Lawrence Bullard. **73** *bottom right* Designer: Jack

Index